MW00423173

ADVANCED PRAISE FOR ANTI-RACISM 4REALS

"*Anti-Racism 4REALS* is an indispensable resource for equipping all who are serious about the work of dismantling racism. It provides a disciplined approach to generating meaningful engagement that will lead to transformative action. Rev. Beckford and Rev. Ledder bring a unique combination of skills and experience to this project. Readers of this excellent book will benefit immensely from their journey." —**Rev. Dr. Richard Hayes, Pastor, Metropolitan Community United Methodist Church**

"Revs. Beckford and Ledder move the needle and raise the bar for those committed to the urgent work of anti-racism. In this candid, provocative, incisive book, we are pushed and prodded to transcend talk, neutrality, political correctness, and our need for more information about racism; we are challenged to take up specific, real-time strategies that interrupt and dismantle racism, hold space for honest truth-telling, and lead to real action and real change. *Anti-Racism 4Reals* offers a practical blueprint for the future of anti-racism work."—**Mark Feldmeir, pastor and author of *A House Divided***

"We don't need more talk about race: we need real talk about race. Sheila M. Beckford and E. Michelle Ledder have created a highly accessible resource to help you and your community move beyond polite words to real talk that makes a real difference. In this critical time of real danger and real opportunity, we need to get real."—**Brian D. McLaren, author of *Faith After Doubt***

"*Anti-Racism 4REALS* is an intense yet insightful read! Discovering how certain words and actions can unknowingly perpetrate racism and making a conscious decision to change them are essential components to building an anti-racist culture. This book helps you learn how to take the big and small steps needed to do this important work."—**Leah Gunning Francis, author of *Ferguson and Faith: Sparking Leadership and Awakening Community***

"The authors of this book offer thought provoking ideas and commentary on the importance of race, diversity, and inclusion. In the 21st century, it is absolutely imperative and mission critical that we work to achieve equity, while engaging in bold, daring, courageous, and honest conversations regarding the issue of race and its debilitating impact on the promotion of human flourishing. Further, this book helps us to see that it takes diversity of all dimensions to create a truly global, transformational, and equitable society. The authors do an incredibly amazing job unpacking complicated concepts and teasing out the nuances—so that readers are provided with the tools they need to be effective agents of change in progressively addressing and dismantling the system of white domination and superiority in all spheres of the human endeavor."—**Rev. Dr. Herron Keyon Gaston, author of *The Darkest Night: An Incarceration Memoir, from Jail to Yale***

ANTI-RACISM
4REALS

REAL TALK

WITH

REAL STRATEGIES

IN

REAL TIME

FOR

REAL CHANGE

SHEILA M. BECKFORD & E. MICHELLE LEDDER

**chalice
press**

Saint Louis, Missouri

An imprint of Christian Board of Publication

Cover art and design: 99 Designs

Interior design: Overcup

ChalicePress.com

PRINT: 9780827201026
EPUB: 9780827201033
EPDF: 9780827201040

Printed in the United States of America

Table of Contents

Acknowledgements

We, the Reverends Sheila M. Beckford and E. Michelle Ledder, were called and destined to do this anti-racist anti-racism work together. We spoke about creating this book in August of 2019 and were granted a contract with Chalice Press in November 2020.

We, 4REALS, would like to acknowledge those who were instrumental in bringing this valuable work to life. The formal and informal legal, publishing, accounting, and editorial support we have received throughout this project has helped us in numerous ways to realize our dream to become published authors. We are grateful.

Sheila M. Beckford

I would like to thank **my ancestors** who nurtured this passion for justice within me.

My mother, the Diva, **Greta C. Beckford**, taught me to be a person who lives in my truth and not up to others' expectations of me. You taught me that community is essential to ensuring justice and freedom reign. Your spirit lives within me. Thank you, Mami!

The **Reverend Dr. Vincent Harding**, one of my spiritual Fathers, helped me to better understand and offered me an insightful perspective into the work of the Civil Rights Movement. Your patience and corrective measures were filled with the love of a father and a friend.

I will forever love you both and hope to make you proud. Rest in Power!

To my **Sankofa Sistahs**, I am blessed because of your gifts of love and justice. We will continue to live into our purpose as we educate and agitate an injustice system's conscience.

To **Tiffany French Goffe and Reverend Marcia White-Smith**, thanks for recognizing my potential as an author.

To my spiritual parents **Rev. Pauline Wardell-Sankoh** and the **Reverend Dr. William G. Smartt**, you nurtured me and loved me back to health.

To **Yvette Zeno**, who cares for me, supports me, and encourages me when I need it most, thank you!

To **Rev. Dorlimar Lebron Malave**, my right hand, thanks for all the times you sacrificed your schedule to care for Zai.

To the **Hayes family**, the **Reverend Dr. Richard, Mrs. Bridget**, and **Issa**: Thank you for instituting the family game nights that allowed Zai and me to woosah, and for the indescribable bond forged in life-giving laughter, competitiveness, and smack-talking.

To **my family the McField, Ebanks, and Beckford clan** – thank you to those who are always proud of me and celebrate all of my accomplishments. To **my nephew, Karl**, who holds me down, checks on me regularly, challenges me, corrects me in love, and responded to my news of writing this book with, "that's dope!" you are the real MVP!

To **my eldest Cheyenne**, you are my biggest cheerleader!

And to my daughter **Zai**, who gave up some movie nights and became my "meeting reminder" so I could complete this project. You are my world!

E. Michelle Ledder

I would like to deeply thank all the historic and contemporary **Church Mothers and Grandmothers** who never knew me personally but prayed for "all of those who don't know Jesus." This was me, until my midtwenties. Your prayers brought this now-ordained person from the muck and mire so that God could start me on my way. I am forever grateful—because you didn't have to do it, but you did.

To the **innumerable Black people and others who have been direct targets of racism**, who have shared their lives and experiences with me, in front of me, and in public spaces. I hold these testimonies as sacred and in both my mind's eye and soul as I write and do this work. All of what I know about anti-racism has come explicitly or implicitly from BIPAL people. I am indebted beyond measure – and pray what I do and say is honorable in your sight.

To the **Reverend Dr. Eric Severson**, thank you for not trying to make me into a mini-you but rather honoring the skills and wisdom God gave me so I could live into my own academic prowess and vocational authenticity. Thank you for showing me what it looks like when a white person does anti-racism work honorably. It was then I first recognized my life's work.

To the **Reverend Dr. Teresa Fry Brown,** words could never be enough to express my gratitude to you and for you. Thank you for teaching me preaching lessons, teaching lessons, AME lessons, and life lessons. Thank you for always knowing the exact perfect timing for when to push the tissue box over and when to push me beyond my limiting thoughts. Thank you for modeling what it looks like to stare evil and sin right in the face, turn them to dust, and retain ALL your dignity. I pray my work honors you and provides a legacy of which you are proud.

4REALS

To the **Reverend Dr. Leslie Duroseau** and the **Reverend Dr. Gregory Ellison**, who helped to name us and our project. We recognized more fully who we could become because you saw what we did not yet see. Your guidance and care-filled words of encouragement, insight, and creativity helped to elevate 4REALS to new heights. We are so grateful to walk alongside you both and are excited for what the future holds.

We do this work in the **name and Spirit of the Liberator**—the one who is both love and justice but never erases one for the other.

To the Reader

We thank you for entering into this work to
address racism in very REAL ways.

This book was written with all of you in mind.

Though our backgrounds include and are primarily based in
church contexts, you will find the 4REALS templates and
examples easily translatable into your context.

We deeply appreciate the on-the-ground wisdom that you,
the reader, bring to this work.

4REALS brings truly anti-racist anti-racism practices to life with
one hundred and thirty-seven strategies and skills.

You bring the contextual wisdom needed for this work
to become REAL where you are.

Let us enter the not only important but critical work of anti-racism together:

REAL TALK with REAL STRATEGIES in REAL TIME for REAL CHANGE.

Introduction

That First Meeting—Racialized Terror, Racial Positionality, Real Anti-Racism

In May 2019, the Reverends Sheila M. Beckford and E. Michelle Ledder met for the first time in the aftermath of racialized terror. The circumstances were unusual but not unique. A prominent, mostly white social justice board of directors had gathered at a retreat center in Maryland—but not for the reasons one might first imagine. Earlier that year, one of its white directors had perpetrated a series of racist acts upon Black people who gathered at a United Methodist national conference to oppose social oppression of another group. The board convened in May to address what had happened and to figure out what they needed to do to repair their reputation and "become anti-racist." The fallout of the incidents had been wide and swift. Local branches of the denomination's Black and Latino/x caucuses had publicly denounced the social justice group and declared unapologetically that they would no longer work with them. The publicity of this explicit break in working relationship as well as the details and whispers of the racism enacted sent waves of public judgment upon the Christian social justice group, which was otherwise known for its LGBTQIA full-inclusion activism.

Rev. Beckford, a Black woman and chair of the New York Black Caucus, was one of the Black people who was targeted by the racist acts. She was there to provide her testimony, to name exactly what happened as one way to challenge the board of directors to deal directly with what they had done. Rev. Ledder, a white woman and Director of Equity and Anti-Racism for the denomination's agency on race, was there to highlight the racism and the effects of the racism brought forward from Rev. Beckford's and other Black leaders' experiences. Rev. Beckford and Rev. Ledder named racism in straightforward ways—Rev. Beckford as a Black woman who was targeted by and has fought against racism her whole life, and Rev. Ledder as a white woman who was there to teach the white board members the specifics of the racism they enacted and a way toward becoming an anti-racist organization. What began as a one-time dialogue about racism with a Christian social justice board of directors turned into an ongoing friendship and working partnership that highlights honest, insightful, incisive, and increasingly generative conversations and cofacilitated workshops about racism and anti-racism.

Unfortunately, the above scenario represents not an anomaly but instead one pervasive form of racism—that which stems from Christian organizations that are social justice-based and white-dominant in leadership, content, and strategy. Just proclaiming Christianity, faith, or justice-focused intent does not immunize people or organizations from perpetrating or being targeted by racism. Leadership positions do not miraculously create leaders with the know-how and skill sets to create racial equity and justice. In other words, anti-racism doesn't happen by chance, even in the Church—perhaps especially there.

WRITE, DRAW, OR NOTE YOUR RESPONSES BELOW: *What were your initial responses to reading that the racialized terror incident above was perpetrated by a white leader of a Christian social justice organization against Black members of their own denomination? Were you surprised? Not surprised? Why?*

While it is easy to say that the Church is made up of people who struggle and sin, more often than not Christians have created a utopian sense of what Church could be or should be and so are doubly disappointed when we so disastrously fall short. We understandably want the Church to be the place and the places where racism no longer exists, where people can fully and authentically be free without the evils of white supremacy. We want the Church to be the model of what it looks like when God's dreams for humanity and the world come true and the lion and the lamb chill out with one another in true Shalom. When the people and organizations of the Church perpetrate and are targeted by racism, a little bit of our spirit dies, collapsing under the weight of yet another disillusionment and of occluded potential.

So, we search for language and rituals taught to us by sacred texts and traditions enacted over centuries to attempt to live into who we've been created and called to be. We highlight our belief that all people have been created in the image of God. We center dialogues with one another and across lines of racial difference (which is often just called "diversity") for the purpose of understanding and building relationships. We latch onto Jesus' sayings about forgiveness and attempt to figure out what it means to be a "good" Christian in the midst of harm perpetrated even by one's Christian siblings. However, many times the Church and her people are bogged down by "church-nice" or "church-polite" or even "church-mean" language that gets us nowhere. Worse still, there remain Church teachings that in many contexts create the kin-dom of God here on earth, but when said and enacted in the midst of racial terror and injustice actually perpetrate racism. Fortunately, we need not rid ourselves of the Church or our faith to do the work of anti-racism. What we need are anti-racism tools and interpretive lenses to help us see *how* the sacred texts and traditions of our faith lead us directly and faithfully into anti-racism work and lives.

One foundational lens that is necessary for anti-racism work but countered often by Church teachings is racial positionality.[1] The church teaches

---

[1] The Reverend E. Michelle Ledder first used the term *racial positionality* to describe racial identity within the system of racism while working at the General Commission on Religion and Race (GCORR) of the United Methodist Church (2016 to present). While she hadn't heard the term *racial positionality* before, it entered her thinking emerging from concepts and pedagogies taught to her by her advisor, the Reverend Dr. Teresa Fry Brown. Many examples exist, but two are listed here. Some years ago, Dr. Fry Brown imagined a book written by the two of them—from different racial identities, different vocational standpoints, and different Christian journeys—about their experiences in the AME church. It is quite possible this conversation is what planted the seeds for Rev. Ledder's connection with this

a model of equality that flattens out differences in order to highlight our similarities. However, the realities of race and racism create different consequences for people based on our racial markers. Within the system of racism, white people are prioritized, privileged, and protected while BIPAL (Black, Indigenous, Pacific-Islander, Asian, and Latino/x)[2] people are dehumanized, disenfranchised, and discriminated against. Just like the four gospels have different perspectives, focus areas, and wisdom based on the contextual realities of their authors, so also do we based on our racialized contextual realities. Racial positionality signifies the very real but symbolic spheres within which BIPAL people and white folks exist within the system of racism. In other words, the term helps us keep in the forefront how people of different races experience the world differently because of the system of racism. The Church often gets anti-racism work wrong because we attempt to use a language of equality (similarity) to discuss, describe, and dismantle a system based in difference. What we need are words and actions that retain the divine dream of equality while addressing the realities of difference inherent in the system of racism.

White people are crying out more and more, "What can I do?" But they are in deep need of anti-racist strategies that do not perpetrate racism. BIPAL people need strategies to combat the inherent consequences of racism—interpersonal and institutional racism, internalized racism—and strategies for how to hold white allies accountable without capitulating to racist ideologies. In such a time as this, it is increasingly necessary to provide models and options for anti-racism that refuse to rely on temporary fixes. We believe that *Anti-Racism 4REALS: Real Talk with Real Strategies in Real Time for Real Change* is one model capable of moving faith-based and good-intended people from thoughts and prayers to the real strategies that bring about real change in real time.

---

book's template of responses based in racial positionality. Also, Dr. Fry Brown's pedagogy of preaching emphasizes God calling preachers to preach from their own voices and not another's. This deep respect for authenticity protects space for sermons to be enriched by the different questions we ask or different ways God gifts each of us uniquely. For Rev. Ledder, both of these main ideas create a perfect backdrop for her thinking about how each of us is positioned differently within the system of racism, with different experiences, perspectives, and wisdom (or lack of it) because of it.

[2] Many articles reference People of Color (PoC) or Black, Indigenous, and People of Color (BIPOC) to avoid centering whiteness when describing racial identity. The Reverend Sheila M. Beckford uses the term BIPAL (Black, Indigenous, Pacific-Islanders, Asian, and Latino/x) to represent multiple racial identities by naming them separately to further decenter whiteness in discussions of anti-racism and beyond.

What We Need is Real Talk, Not More Talk, about Racism and Anti-Racism

Much of our focus as Christians who want to do anti-racism work is on dialogues. We want to talk with one another instead of at one another. We want to understand each other better. We want to unlock that which we don't know in order to provide us with the answers we so desperately need. Dialogue in and of itself is not the problem. Dialogues that result only in more talk are the problem. But what does it mean to have *real talk* about racism and anti-racism versus just *more talk*? We thought we'd put our own work to work by sharing our thoughts with you using the anti-racism foundational lens of racial positionality. What follows are separate responses by Rev. Sheila M. Beckford (a Black woman United Methodist pastor) and Rev. E. Michelle Ledder (a white woman African Methodist Episcopal minister). Each of us will respond not only based in our racial positionality but make the connections between what we say and our racial positionality as clear as possible. The reasoning for this is multifold: It helps us, as writers, keep our own racial positionality at the forefront, which helps us to do anti-racism work well; it helps to create clear connections for you, the reader, between anti-racism work and racial identity; and it foreshadows the structure of the book ahead.

So, let's try it. The prompt is this: What does it mean to have REAL TALK, not more talk, about racism and anti-racism?

REV. BECKFORD'S RESPONSE: In the Black community, the phrase *REAL TALK* means giving it to you straight with no filter, no hiding behind respectability politics or politeness. Respectability politics occurs when BIPAL people are directed by those in their same group to assimilate to the dominant group in order to be accepted. We are told that if we just follow the rules, get our education, dress well, and speak well, we will be protected from harm by white wrath. For example, recently someone shared a meme. The top photo included the Reverend Dr. Martin Luther King Jr., Rev. Abernathy, and others marching arm in arm, dressed in suits and trench coats. The image on the bottom of the meme featured young men wearing pants that sagged. In between the two images a caption read, "They respected this [the top image] and not this." My REAL TALK response beneath the post stated, "The Reverend Dr. Martin Luther King Jr. was assassinated anyhow."

In the spring of 2020, the world viewed the murders of Ahmaud Arbery (Georgia) and George Floyd (Minnesota). We were infuriated by the killings of Breonna Taylor (Kentucky) and Elijah McClain (Colorado) In response, white people sought ways to understand their own racism. Many sought answers by reading books, while others sought to find the answers by asking (in fact, demanding) for BIPAL people, especially Black people, to educate them. Although some of the materials were great reads and allowed people to form book studies, they lacked something essential; their talk remained just that: talk. BIPAL, especially Black and Indigenous people, are tired of talk without change. We are tired of hearing talk that leads to more talk but not to action. REAL TALK requires action.

Churches need REAL TALK, not more talk. While serving in a predominately white church, a white parishioner made the following statement: "I don't see your color." Immediately, I corrected her, saying, "I am a big, tall, Black woman with an afro; you better see my color." I continued to explain to her that to deny seeing my color is called erasure. White people do this to erase the part of a person that makes them uncomfortable in an effort to feel comfortable with an individual or group. Of course, this interruption of her racist statement made her and other white people in the room uncomfortable because they had never experienced REAL TALK. Many white people who were there spoke with me after the meeting, and for months afterward shared with me their displeasure at my public response. They told me I should have educated her without publicly embarrassing her. More talk pulls white people to the side to discuss their racism in private. REAL TALK interrupts harm in the moment. More talk allows people to remain where they are. REAL TALK requires action steps, such as white people holding each other accountable for their racism. More talk may show intellectual "wokeness" but no reparative actions. More talk promotes harm; REAL TALK interrupts harm.

> *More talk promotes harm*
> *REAL TALK interrupts harm*

REV. LEDDER'S RESPONSE: For those of us who are white, we are consistent in finding ways to distract ourselves from having to do our hard work of anti-racism. Having more talk about racism and anti-racism instead of REAL TALK is one such diversion. The reasons for this abound and, at this point, don't matter. The outcome is that, in terms of anti-racism work, those of us who are white must develop the capability and the motivation to reduce our racism, which pries our attention and energy away from anti-racist strategies. Ironically, avoiding REAL TALK by using dialogue is one distraction.

One way white people misinterpret, misuse, and misappropriate anti-racism strategies created by BIPAL people is by co-opting dialogues. Whether dialogues are in the form of book studies, workshops/trainings, small group conversations, or relationship-building over food, those of us who are white consistently use these opportunities for more talk rather than REAL TALK about racism and anti-racism. We do this in numerous ways, including but not limited to the following:

- We take up all the space in conversations: White folks will fill the space of anti-racism talk with our experiences, our feelings, and our strategies. We either feel too uncomfortable to deal with our own culpability or too inadequate to do something meaningful, and to compensate we fill the space with our words. The white supremacist notion that white people's ideas and feelings should fill any and all spaces (even those dedicated to anti-racism) perpetuates racism: more talk.

- We create talk "about" racism/anti-racism without action: Have you ever attended a meeting that gathers solely to discuss the previous meeting without providing next steps or new ideas? In anti-racism work, this translates to book studies that lead to discussions but not to action; workshop hoarding that makes those of us who are white feel better but that does nothing to change our methods or behavior; or quoting facts about racism (or anti-racism strategies) without enacting them in tangible, meaningful, or powerful ways according to BIPAL people. More talk.

- We develop our own anti-racism task forces or strategies: When those of us who are white create our own anti-racism strategies without taking our guidance from BIPAL people, we only create more talk. We are duplicating (badly) the efforts of BIPAL people who already have strategies in place that we can learn to support responsibly. When white people believe we are the ones to create anti-racism strategies, we perpetrate the racism that teaches us that white people always have the answer. More subtle excuses for this racism sound like "I want to use my position of power to create change" or "I wanted to do the proper research for a sound course of action."

REAL TALK is always anti-racist—it *actually* interrupts and dismantles racism. More talk about racism and anti-racism reifies the status quo and generates new expressions of racism all the while. For example, REAL TALK implores those of us who are white to utilize the book study to enact the anti-racism strategies that emerge from its pages. REAL TALK is also anti-racist in **both** content and method. More talk can be anti-racist in one while perpetrating racism in another. For example, attending a protest against police brutality against Black people is anti-racist in content. White people attending the protest and talking to reporters instead of guiding them toward Black activists is racist in method.

> *Matthew 18:15–17a (CEB)*
>
> *"If your [sibling] sins against you, go and correct them when you are alone together. If they listen to you, then you've won over your [sibling]. But if they won't listen, take with you one or two others so that every word may be established by the mouth of two or three witnesses. But if they still won't pay attention, report it to the church."*

Rev. Beckford's response noted that often in anti-racism work, talk gets REAL when racism is called out in the moment. It matters not whether the racism is considered blatant or subtle; the white person who is made aware of their racism becomes embarrassed or ashamed and reacts. Placing the burden of responsibility on the person who named the racism rather than the one who perpetrated it, the text about taking your sibling aside in private is interpreted to mean that the "calling out of racism" should also be done in private. However, this interpretation does not apply in anti-racism work. This is because the above text refers to a sin that has occurred between only two people. "If your sibling sins against you …" Racism enacted in front of others has happened in public. The harm has already been done against people of color, and REAL TALK, the only people who probably aren't aware of it are the white folks. Thus, the call for a private consult over someone's racism is invoked to protect white people's feelings. (Sometimes, BIPAL people invoke this, too—part of the reason is that internalized racism teaches BIPAL people to want to protect white people's feelings!)

We'll be focusing on role-plays to interrupt racism in the REAL TIME chapter, but for now, how does the above reinterpretation help you understand how REAL TALK can be used to interrupt racism in the moment and why it's important? How does your racial identity influence how you're thinking about this right now?

Chapter 1:

4REALS: Real Talk with Real Strategies in Real Time for Real Change

Anti-Racism 4REALS is both an anti-racist template and an anti-racism organization. The term *anti-racism* assumes as true the reality of racism to survive and thrive in environments without intentional and explicit actions and actors capable of disrupting, dismantling, and destroying it. Racism will not surrender to the weak calls for gradual change that are beholden to the timeline of those who are racially protected. Rather, racism is fortified by such efforts—it relishes in its ability to bathe in the tepid waters of compromise and consciences that are comfortable with accepting the suffering of others as collateral damage. Anti-racism is anything that *actually* interrupts and dismantles racism.

> ### *Anti-Racism is anything that ACTUALLY interrupts and dismantles racism*

The question is, how do we do that? Anti-Racism 4REALS literally suggests four (4) REALS.

In this book, we will utilize several strategies and approaches to developing REAL TALK about racism, which ultimately means action and change. The following describes the components of this book and what to expect as you work through it.

REAL TALK finds every way possible to use words to interrupt and dismantle racism. Have you ever been part of discussions about racism and anti-racism that are so shallow and superficial that you might as well have been talking about the weather or the local sports team? There are many conversations that never get to what is needed to interrupt and dismantle racism. Even dialogues with titles that include words like *diversity*, *racial justice*, *racial reconciliation* (whatever that's supposed to mean!), or *anti-racism* can fall short when they do not get at what needs to be said and how it needs to be said.

The corporate world teaches its leaders to speak in neutral terms to maintain professionalism. Schools hide behind political correctness, which allows false objectivity to masquerade as facts. The Church also fails hard at this because many of us have been taught that in order to be a Christian, we must always be polite/nice/gentle/compassionate/loving. The problems are not the terms or inclinations themselves but how they are interpreted and lived out while addressing oppression—in this case, racism. For example, *polite* and *nice* become code words for "Don't say anything that gets white people upset." *Gentle* transforms into soft-pedaling around difficult issues rather than directly naming them. *Compassionate* translates to understanding racism as someone's opinion or upbringing rather than addressing the oppression and injustice. *Loving* is described as "meeting people where they are" but ends up leaving racists where they are until they feel comfortable enough to change, if ever. (By the way, if that sentence was difficult for you to read, it may be because you've been hearing more talk about racism versus anti-racist REAL TALK. We'll go into this more throughout the book!)

REAL TALK not only names racism directly but also says things in ways that enact anti-racist strategies within the content and proclamation of the words themselves. For example, in contrast to "journey language," REAL TALK advocates for "entry point" language.[3] Entry points create a way for all people to start anti-racism work right now. The work of an anti-racism trainer, book, or workshop is to find entry points for people and develop learning engagements that connect someone's entry point (perspective, prior training, learning style, and so on) with the work of anti-racism. Entry point language also removes the literal and symbolic space for people (especially white people) to wiggle out of responsibilities to dismantle racism that journey language permits. REAL TALK

[3] The Reverend E. Michelle Ledder first used "entry point" language to describe places where people do the work of anti-racism while she was working at the General Commission on Religion and Race (GCORR) of the United Methodist Church (2016 to present).

places what is needed for discussions about racism and anti-racism in direct contact with how to say the uncomfortable things, how to do the uncomfortable things, and how to remain faithful and authentically human all the while.

REAL STRATEGIES prioritize ACTION-NOW Learning Engagements to move everyone beyond just talking about racism to immediate anti-racism actions. Rather than relying on models that demand that talk (REAL or otherwise) occur first and in isolation from action, REAL STRATEGIES places action at the center of Anti-Racism 4REALS. If anti-racism is anything that *actually* interrupts and dismantles racism, it just makes sense that actions are necessary. However, so much of current anti-racism practice, especially within the Church, is predicated on talking about and agreeing on truth of content, strategies necessary, and actions in order to engage. Book studies abound as new information is published and church groups gather in unprecedented numbers after the racialized terror murders of George Floyd, Ahmaud Arbery, Breonna Taylor, and Elijah McClain in 2020. But how many of those book studies have created any, let alone sustainable, change for racial justice or equity? How many book studies create tangible, meaningful, and powerful anti-racism acts? Instead, how many book studies led to quoting truths *about* racism and anti-racism without *actually* interrupting and dismantling it?

ACTION-NOW Learning Engagements are exercises that bridge the gap between learning about something and doing something. Anti-Racism 4REALS believes that all people can begin doing anti-racism now, and in three (3) steps or less. REAL STRATEGIES interrupts and dismantles the workshop-hoarder mentality that believes attending workshops can be equated with anti-racism work or that one more workshop will "get me ready" to do what's necessary. REAL STRATEGIES also breaks the chains of information-only workshops—even at the introductory entry point— by creating processes by which action can be taken right now. For example, have you ever been in the presence of someone making a racist joke? How did you respond? Did you interrupt them? Did you stay silent? Did you leave? Did you laugh? REAL STRATEGIES moves from learning and talking about anti-racism work to the actual doing of reparative racial justice.

REAL STRATEGIES are placed at the end of every chapter—including this introduction—so that the work of anti-racism begins without a waiting period. Each will be based on a threefold template of THE BIG IDEA (what you learn about in the chapter), ACTION-NOW (for immediate use), and ENTRY POINTS (racial positionality and prior skill set). Without REAL STRATEGIES even the realest of REAL TALK becomes just more talk. Book studies which have the potential to dismantle racist thinking will actually lead to anti-racist acts instead of dialogues about the dialogues. Missed opportunities to interrupt racism will decrease as we learn how information becomes the actions that bolster our courage, resistance, and conviction. REAL STRATEGIES make REAL TALK real.

REAL TIME incorporates role-plays so that people can practice scripts and rehearse plans in preparation to interrupt and dismantle racism in the moment. REAL TALK and REAL STRATEGIES can't interrupt and dismantle racism if when the racism occurs we can't enact them. Racism happens in real time, so anti-racism must also happen in REAL TIME. Anti-Racism 4REALS recognizes that even prepared anti-racists will experience situations when racism occurs and the words or interruptions won't come. This is for many reasons. Sometimes, for those of us who are white, the momentum of our inaction has yet to be overcome, or we recognize the racism but don't have a skill set necessary to interrupt it or dismantle it. For BIPAL people, at times the act of racism itself is so hurtful that the trauma of the event necessitates self-care without overt disruption. Sometimes, BIPAL people wait for white people to step up and take responsibility for the anti-racism they purport to be about. At other times, internalized oppression creates in BIPAL people the need to protect white people or shield them from their own embarrassment even as they perpetrate racism.

But REAL TIME isn't restricted to racism that occurs "out there." 4REALS, as an organization, believes that anti-racism isn't simply information that is taught but the method by which the work is done. 4REALS believes that REAL TIME begins in the learning (even during anti-racism workshops or books) and that there are faithful ways to address racism even at the introductory entry points. Interrupting racism in anti-racism workshops has the power to model what faithful Christianity, humanity, and anti-racism work looks and sounds like in REAL TIME. These same strategies can be used to provide a model for interrupting racism in churches, schools, at work, at home, and most, if not all settings.

CAUTION: Anti-racists *only* role-play the interruption of the racism, not the racism itself, because this mitigates to the best of our ability the harms of racism. We do not perpetrate racism in real time in order to interrupt racism in REAL TIME. (For white folks reading this and wondering how to become better at recognizing racism in real time without role-plays, use a Google search. Unfortunately, plenty of examples of every type of racism abound.)

REAL CHANGE crafts accountability templates and measures to ensure that tangible, meaningful, and powerful change for racial justice replaces good intentions and workshops. REAL CHANGE requires that we focus on outcome, not on intent. There is often a disconnectedness between intent and what actually occurs. One reason for this is racialized implicit bias, but other factors impede REAL CHANGE as well. Some organizations attempt to do anti-racism work using the "add-on" method, which retains a foundation of white supremacy and "adds" trainings or special days on top. Some leaders are so entrenched in the way things are because that's how they got there.

Anti-racism 4REALS defines anti-racism as anything that *actually* interrupts and dismantles racism. REAL CHANGE provides ways to track, assess, and analyze successes and failures (yes, failures), and make on-the-go shifts that avoid the most common roadblocks and obstacles to anti-racism work. REAL CHANGE creates methods of accountability and transparency that build not only timelines and momentum but also trust. *Change* is a word that has been cheapened by superficial and temporary fixes that might feel good to some in the moment but that do nothing to shift the ethos of an institution or the commitment of an individual. REAL CHANGE provides the external measurements and an accountability paradigm that brings all people the opportunity to participate in anti-racism work that actually does the work of anti-racism.

Chapter Outline: Two Responses and an ACTION-NOW Learning Engagement

Rev. Beckford and Rev. Ledder have created a way to model what REAL TALK with REAL STRATEGIES in REAL TIME about racism and anti-racism can mean for REAL CHANGE. Each chapter will highlight one REAL one aspect of racism or anti-racism, and will include three sub-sections: a response from Rev. Beckford; a response from Rev. Ledder; and a collective response based in an anti-racist skill/action the reader can use right away. In-book journaling with prompt questions (as you've already seen) will continue to create the literal space for any reader to move beyond just absorbing material to internalizing the internal and external work necessary for anti-racism.

The chapter on REAL TALK focuses on the role of silence in its multiple forms—repressive or oppressive, vigilant or violent, protective or as a means of survival. The REAL STRATEGIES chapter highlights how racial positionality influences which actions white allies and BIPAL people should engage. Included also is a chart with eight sets of scenarios and multiple entry points for immediate use. REAL TIME gets right to the point prioritizing doing the work of interrupting and dismantling racism and the obstructions that get in the way. Chapter 4 on REAL CHANGE includes a list of things anti-racists should stop right now as well as accountability measures and templates for anti-racist outcomes. Finally, the conclusion presents an overarching anti-racism strategy that honors racial positionality and creates a method for challenging white folks to do the anti-racism work needed without placing a double burden on BIPAL people.

ACTION-NOW Learning Engagement—Doing Anti-Racism Work Responsibly

Anti-Racism 4REALS believes that at every moment, every person can do anti-racism work. This is why we've included critical journal prompts even in the introduction and why now we're providing an ACTION-NOW Learning Engagement that provides an anti-racism skill you can use as soon as you read it. It's called anti-racist covenants.[4]

Anti-racist covenants can be seen as corrections to safe space or even brave space covenants: lists of pre-agreed-upon ways of speaking and being with one another when having difficult conversations or working alongside each other across lines of difference. Safe space covenants were created to try to literally create spaces where people felt safe enough to be vulnerable with others different from themselves. Soon, however, cri-

---

[4] The Reverend E. Michelle Ledder first created a version of anti-racist covenants while working at the General Commission on Religion and Race (GCORR) for the United Methodist Church. The first versions were inspired by attending a meeting hosted by the Young People's Department of the Washington DC NAACP, who introduced a dialogue agreement created by groups caucused by race. The current version included here has been adapted and modified by 4REALS: Anti-Racist Anti-Racism Training and Consulting, LLC.

tiques of these attempts emerged as participants realized it was impossible to create full safety. Brave space covenants attempt to rectify this by replacing the impossible goal of safety with the possibility of creating spaces where people could be brave enough to be vulnerable even though 100 percent safety couldn't be achieved. However, both safe space and brave space covenants fall into the same trap: They still prioritize the dominant or protected group.

Racism works just like all other spheres of oppression. Within a system of oppression, there are those who are protected, prioritized, and privileged, and those who are discriminated against and who are the direct targets of the oppression. Within the system of racism, white people are the protected group and BIPAL people are the direct targets. More than the inability of any covenant items to provide 100 percent safety, the limitations of safe space and brave space covenants lie in their replication of the dominant group's worldview and the protection of their safety and comfort. Here, we're including three (3) anti-racist covenant items so that you, the reader, can start doing REAL TALK the very next time your anti-racism group/workshop leader initiates a covenant to determine how the work will proceed.

The following table has three columns. The first represents the goal of the covenant item. The second column represents how you might see it written in a safe space or brave space covenant. The final column shows language for an anti-racist covenant item. Outcomes are listed for the safe/brave space item and the anti-racist item. Notice how the outcomes of the safe/brave space items get away from the stated goal while the anti-racist covenant items point more closely toward it. Notice your reactions to reading them. If you are white, take special care to think about how the safe/brave space item has protected you in the past. If you are a BIPAL person, think about how, if at all, the anti-racist covenant item would mitigate the harm of the safe/brave spaces you've been part of in the past. If you believe it wouldn't, what language would help it to do that? For everyone, name at least one specific thing you can do to live out one of the anti-racist covenant items the next time you are doing anti-racist work.

GOAL	SAFE/BRAVE SPACE COVENANT	ANTI-RACIST COVENANT
Recognize that everyone comes to anti-racism work from different experiences.	Assume everyone has good intentions. (Outcome: White people believe that intent erases harm done by racism.)	Assume humanity / build trust. (Outcome: everyone's humanity is assumed to be true; but white people recognize it is their job to always be working to build the trust necessary for BIPAL people to be vulnerable about race/racism with them; white people never expect to be trusted just because they are in an anti-racism space.)
Anti-racism work is hard and will probably be uncomfortable at least some of the time.	Be challenged to be uncomfortable. (Outcome: Experiences of discomfort between BIPAL people and white people are flattened as if the harm from racism is the same as that of the growing awareness of responsibility for perpetrating it.)	Do our own work and take on intentional challenges. (Outcome: Everyone will be challenged in different ways depending on their racial positionality; BIPAL people might be challenged to trust that anything will change by engaging anti-racism work with white people, while white people will be challenged to take responsibility for their racism without demanding that BIPAL people care for them.)
Treat one another with dignity and respect while working through the realities of racism and responsibilities for anti-racism.	Be polite and respect one another. (Outcome: People use "good-sounding" words to silence resistance or challenges to racism; or REAL TALK is silenced for just "more talk.")	Recognize and avoid using "good-sounding" words that actually do harm: that is, civil, polite, calm, and even nonviolence in some cases. (Outcome: more REAL TALK and less "more talk.")

FOR WHITE FOLKS: How has one safe/brave space item above specifically protected you in anti-racism spaces in the past?

FOR BIPAL PEOPLE: How, if at all, would an anti-racist item above specifically mitigate the harm a safe/brave space item has done? If not at all, what language would you change?

FOR ALL: What specific way will you enact one anti-racist covenant item above?

Chapter 2:

REAL TALK

The first of the four REALS, REAL TALK, has been defined as that which finds every way possible to use words to interrupt and dismantle racism. REAL TALK not only names racism directly but also says things in ways that enact anti-racist strategies within the content and proclamation of the words themselves. REAL TALK creates opportunities for every person to engage in anti-racism right away. It places what is needed for discussions about racism and anti-racism in direct contact with how to say the uncomfortable things, how to do the uncomfortable things, and how to remain faithful and authentically human all the while.

In this chapter, we'll delve more deeply into REAL TALK by focusing on the anti-racism reality that "silence is violence." Our racially positioned responses will include REAL TALK in at least three ways: [1] REAL TALK about "silence is violence" as an anti-racism strategy; [2] REAL TALK about how racism co-opts "silence is violence" to perpetrate more racism; and [3] how REAL TALK can be used to help all of us do anti-racism work by considering a "horizon of silence" as the foundation for this chapter's ACTION-NOW Learning Engagement. Let's begin ...

REV. BECKFORD'S RESPONSE: Before you go any further, take a moment to think about your organization's no-tolerance-for-violence policy.

WRITE YOUR RESPONSE BELOW: *What definitions or words come to mind while reflecting on your organization's no-tolerance-for-violence policy?*

Organizations institute no-tolerance-for-violence policies and enforce them with rigorous punishments. School systems suspend or expel students, while employers terminate employees. However, these same institutions' best practices protect and perpetuate violence through silence. Have you ever heard the phrase "silence is violence," or "white silence is racial violence"?

In many instances, when white people witness racialized terror enacted against their Black, Indigenous, Pacific-Islander, Asian, and Latino/x colleagues—especially their Black and Indigenous colleagues—they are silent until there is an opportunity to speak with the target one-on-one. This is the time when they express how the act was "wrong," or how the tone or rhetoric spewed was offensive "even to" them. However, they were silent at the moment because it was beneficial to remain in the system.

In his book study, Dr. Walter Brueggemann highlights how silence can perpetrate violence within organizational systems: "Silence is a complex matter. It can refer to awe before unutterable holiness, but it can also refer to coercion where some voices are silenced in the interest of control by the dominant voices."[5] Brueggemann refers to this as "repressive silence."

Many organizations build on ideologies that benefit white people. Often, the dominant groups' ideas and concepts are accepted, silencing BIPAL

---

[5] Walter Brueggermann, Interrupting Silence: God's Command to Speak Out (Louisville, KY: Westminster John Knox Press, 2018), 1.

people. Companies establish diversity and inclusion hiring practices to ensure that they have hired BIPAL managers. However, selection for these leadership positions requires a denial of culture and an assimilation into the dominant white group.

Churches are not exempt from practicing repressive silence—many mainline (read here: white-dominant) denominations institute ministry appointments for BIPAL clergy to serve in predominantly white churches. The United Methodist Church's Book of Discipline lays out the definition and purpose of this practice, which they term Cross-Racial/Cross-Cultural (CR/CC) appointments.

> Cross-racial and cross-cultural appointments are made as a creative response to increasing racial and ethnic diversity in the church and in its leadership. Cross-racial and cross-cultural appointments are appointments of clergy persons to congregations in which the majority of their constituencies are different from the clergy person's own racial/ethnic and cultural background.[6]

However, the process itself promotes racism. Consistently, BIPAL clergy are appointed to white-dominant churches, while white pastors are less likely to be appointed to a BIPAL church, and mostly in cases where their salaries and perks are inflated. Depending on the racial identity of the BIPAL clergyperson and the racial makeup of the congregation, the expressions of racism can be different. For example, in preparation to serve in a predominantly white congregation, a Black clergyperson was given the church version of "the talk."

Without googling or using any other resource, write in the box below your understanding of "the talk."

WRITE YOUR RESPONSE BELOW: *Without googling or using any other resource, write your understanding of "the talk."*

---

[6] United Methodist Church, The Book of Discipline (Nashville: United Methodist Publishing House, 2016), 347.

"The talk" is the epitome of REAL TALK, which takes place when Black families send their children into the world. "The talk" is a protective measure with specific strategies meant to ensure Black children's survival in a white supremacist world. It caters to white people's expectations of Black submissiveness. The Church has co-opted "the talk" not to help Black people's survival but to coerce silence:

- "Do not try to turn the church into a Black church"
- "Dress to impress"
- "Straighten your hair"
- "Be yourself" (REAL TALK translation: "be an imposter")

We are called to ignore our culture and our experiences or to die to oneself to fit in. When any aspect of the clergy's culture is introduced, it is often met with the same response from the congregants: "This is not that kind of church." What this does is repress the experiences, voice, and authenticity of one's call. The same institution that calls us to respond to the gospel's call of justice and love is now calling for Black clergy to be disingenuous. Additionally, denominations treat racialized terror as isolated incidents rather than a systemic problem.

Throughout this book, we will reinforce that the only way to dislodge, disrupt, and dismantle racism is to interrupt it in **REAL TIME**, which includes speaking out and challenging silence. But **REAL TALK**: what if I told you that those of us who are Black, Indigenous, Asian, Pacific-Islanders, and Latino/x participate in perpetuating racism by interrupting white protective silence?

The white dominant culture is often told not to speak first while Black and Indigenous people are present because white voices and ideas are often valued over their BIPAL counterparts. But in some cases when BIPAL people speak first, it primes the conversation, and white thoughts and truths are suppressed, causing racism to hide in plain sight. For example: During an anti-racism training including Black, Indigenous, Asian, Latino/x, and white participants, whenever the facilitator asked a philosophical question, there was an awkward silence. To break the silence, the BI(P)AL participants would respond, and then white people would feel comfortable enough to share their thoughts on the topic. They took their cues as to how to react from the BI(P)AL participants.

After witnessing this a few times, one of the facilitators, a white woman, stood up and gave the following instructions: "For the next question, I am going to require all who identify as a Person of Color, whether Black, Asian, Latino/x, or Indigenous, to respond after our white siblings." The question: "We are asking each of you to name three things of your culture that you take pride in." The white participants responded:

- "I know this may sound offensive, but I take pride in being white"
- "I take pride in my privilege because I can use it to benefit others"
- "I take pride in my heritage" and
- "I cannot imagine what being Black feels like, but I do not want to experience it."

The responses went along in that manner.

The facilitator then said, "Okay, now all of my siblings who were asked to be quiet, please respond to the question."

The responses were:

- "Dance"
- "Food"
- "Community"
- "Family gatherings"
- "Language"
- "Heritage"

The list continued to build in that manner. Once the facilitator started to list the noticeably different responses, one white woman interjected, "Wait, wait, was this a trick question?" Another white woman chimed in, "That is not the question that was asked of us! Had we known, we would have responded differently."

Was this a trick question? Right now, before you read anything else, in your opinion, was it a trick question? Why? Why not?

The question *was* the same. As a matter of fact, look closely at the invitation to respond to the BI(P)AL participants. The question was not posed to the BI(P)AL participants directly. What was different? There was nowhere to hide, and there were no cues to prepare an anti-racist response. The BI(P)AL participants did not provide the white participants with an opportunity to hide or tone down their racism. There were no leading responses for the white participants to use to reshape their thoughts or to shield their racism.

Knowing when silence is interrupting racism and when it is allowing it to hide in plain sight is often difficult. As BIPAL people, we tend to want to ease the discomfort of white people. We often find ourselves protecting the white dominant group by stating, "Oh, they don't know," "That is not what they meant," or "They did not understand the question." We further surrogate ourselves by posing an alternate way or rephrasing the question for their understanding and protection.

Approximately two years after this training, a friend and I were discussing this event. Her response surprised me to the point that my eyes widened involuntarily. She stated that when our white siblings began to question whether they were tricked, she felt bad for them and immediately wanted to offer a defense for them. However, before she spoke, she took a moment to replay what had actually occurred. She shared with me her realization that her first impulse was to justify the white people's indignation. Her thought process went like this:

- "First, I thought maybe the question was a trick question"
- "Then I replayed it in my mind" (with her hand on her head)
- "I then realized that it was the same question that we responded to"
- "No! I'm trippin'"
- "I then told the group that I didn't think this was a trick question"

In this follow-up conversation, I realized that white manipulation (fragility)[7] had attempted to override my friend's own wisdom and the facts! The ideas of the white dominant group had become the litmus test for normalcy. My friend used a process to reclaim her trust in her own instincts—her own eyes, her own ears, and her natural capacity to know the truth.

Silence is violence because the results of repressive or oppressive silence are internalized racism, racism hiding in plain sight, and policies named as anti-racism despite promoting and protecting racism.

REV. LEDDER'S RESPONSE: The phrase "silence is violence" has become almost everyday language in 2020. From anti-racism work to protest signs and activists' challenges to politicians, the phrase evokes action by its reference to inaction. The rhyme scheme flows easily off the tongue and captures the wandering eye of the internet and news media. As a formulation of language itself, it's catchy and powerful. But words are slippery things—they are released into the world with a power of their own, no longer bound to their original authors or speakers.[8] Ironically, as words

---

[7] The term "white manipulation" is used by the Reverend Sheila M. Beckford to more accurately describe the reality of what is widely referred to as white fragility. According to Beckford, the term *white fragility* centers and recenters whiteness by protecting the racism of white victimhood. In contrast, the term *white manipulation* best describes both the outcome and the strategy. In this book, we use the wording "white manipulation (fragility)" because the term *white fragility* is so widely known that we need a connecting piece to help people know which kind of racism is referred to here.

[8] "Words are slippery things" is a phrase Rev. Ledder has heard her former undergrad professor, Rev. Dr. Eric Severson, say many times though it does not appear in any of his published work. Also see, *Nommo*. "In West Africa, the Dogon people of Mali believe that the African concept of Nommo, the power of the spoken word, carries an energy that produces all life and influences everything from destiny to the naming of children. By human utterance or through the spoken word, human beings can invoke a kind of spiritual power. Nommo, the generative power of the spoken word, is the force that gives life to everything. It is present everywhere, and it brings into existence all that is seen and unseen..." Molefi Kete Asante and Ama Mazama, eds., "Nommo," *Encyclopedia of African Religion*, accessed June 20, 2021.

become more commonplace, it's more important to define and describe what they're meant to do.

Before reading my response to the phrase, continue to reflect on your understanding of "silence is violence" below. Consider including the following: [1] how you first heard the phrase; [2] how you currently understand it; and [3] how your racial identity forms how you understand it.

South African archbishop Desmond Tutu made explicit that "if you are neutral in situations of injustice, you have chosen the side of the oppressor."[9]

In other words, there is no neutral ground with injustice. Our actions, speech, decisions, and values will either proliferate injustice or fight for justice; there is no space for neutrality. Rather, attempting to stay neutral only reinforces the injustice already in place and provides fertile ground for it to continue and grow. The non-act of taking no side, Archbishop Tutu implores, in fact takes the side of the injustice.

In general, when the phrase *silence is violence* is used in anti-racism work, it is meant to compel people to speak against the status quo that upholds racism. In other words, the momentum behind the system and expressions of racism in place is so great that silence not only protects it but entrenches it. Staying silent in the face of racism, the phrase argues, neither reduces the violence of racism nor reduces our complicity in it. Rather, the act of staying silent is an act of violence itself, for which we must be accountable.

More specifically, "silence is violence" in anti-racism work is a charge rightfully aimed at those of us who are white, removing any doubts we hold or lies we tell that our silence does nothing or is neutral. When white people remain silent in the face of racism in any of its expressions, we are agreeing with racism and deeming it acceptable. Our proclamations that we disagree with or don't believe as true specific racist words, policies, or practices are irrelevant. The consequences of white people's silence in

---

[9] Desmond Tutu, *Oxford Essential Quotations*, 5th ed. (Oxford University Press, online version 2017), https://www.oxfordreference.com/view/10.1093/acref. The full quote attributed to Bishop Desmond Tutu reads thus: "If you are neutral in situations of injustice, you have chosen the side of the oppressor. If an elephant has its foot on the tail of a mouse and you say that you are neutral, the mouse will not appreciate your neutrality."

response to racism is never anti-racist and is always concretely violent. Moreover, the violence we do with our silence is multifold.

- <u>The violence of the original racism:</u> Our silence becomes an expression of the original racism and thus participates in the original violence

- <u>The violence of betrayal of our identity:</u> Our silence does violence to any claims of being anti-racist, including but not limited to discrediting our promises to fight against racism, exposing our hesitancy to contradict the lies of racism, and highlighting our unwillingness to risk the benefits we receive from racism

- <u>The violence of betrayal of BIPAL people:</u> Our silence alerts BIPAL people to our allegiances to the benefits and protections of racism over their well-being, success, health, and survival (and thus what should be grotesquely evident, any form of friendship or allyship)

- <u>The violence of the compounding consequences of racism as a system:</u> Because the consequences of racism cannot be limited to a one-time cause and effect, our silence generates more and more racism and the violence associated with it

REFLECTIVE INTERNAL INTERROGATION:

WRITE YOUR RESPONSE BELOW: *How have you experienced or partici-pated in the violence of white silence? Remember to think through the lens of your own racial identity.*

Examples of white silence in the face of racism are increasingly plentiful. Let's consider two of them here: one from the meeting room, one from liturgical practices.

An example of the violence of white silence in meetings: In addition to white people allowing racist remarks, stereotypes, and biases to remain unchallenged during meetings, those of us who are white do violence every time we steal the credit for an idea or solution offered by a BIPAL person. Meetings birthed and drenched in the templates of white supremacy, often invisible to those of us who are white, protect decision-makers and influencers who bypass, minimalize, and ignore ideas and solutions offered by BIPAL people, only to marvel at and celebrate the very same words later offered by a white person. When white people refuse to challenge this practice and explicitly or implicitly receive this credit, we are stealing the intellectual and productive labor of BIPAL people. The white people who argue vigilantly about properly cited sources and punishment for plagiarism are some of the same folks who will not recognize the violence of white silence that unjustly credits white people with the creative and concrete labor of BIPAL people. Although BIPAL people have a multitude of reasons for staying silent in the face of racism in white-dominant spaces and meetings, those of us who are white must always speak unless specifically told by a BIPAL person to remain silent.

An example of the violence of church silence: Churches enact the racism described in the last example as well as racism cloaked in church practices. One such practice is offering "thoughts and prayers" in the wake of racialized terror events. Our racial identity plays a significant role here, too.[10]

BIPAL people offer "thoughts and prayers" after racialized terror for multiple reasons, which span from anti-racism to internalized oppression. In these cases, "thoughts and prayers" might be an act of resistance or a way to focus their attention on centering the work and power of a God who repeatedly intervenes in times of deeply entrenched systemic oppression (for example, the Exodus and Apocalyptic texts in Daniel and Revelations). However, at times, services or statements of "thoughts and prayers" reflect assimilation to a white-dominant denomination or a form

---

[10] As a white person, I always understand things through the lens of being white, even as I attempt to do the work of anti-racism. In my work as an anti-racism trainer, I work with and conduct workshops for both white and BIPAL folks. As an ordained Elder in the African Methodist Episcopal Church, I have the privilege of serving in ministry within a historically and unapologetically Black Christian denomination. These experiences of my own, and those that BIPAL people have shared with me, inform how I understand the strategies and reasoning behind the "thoughts and prayers" response to racialized terror events, as well as how I understand anti-racism work generally.

of internalized oppression that prioritizes the comfort over the account-ability of white people.

REAL TALK, though: For those of us who are white, every expression of "thoughts and prayers" that excludes very specific action-oriented an-ti-racist strategies is racist, and thus violent. Although thoughts and prayers literally say something, they are part of white silence because they do not do the work of anti-racism that concretely makes a change. When those of us who are white offer our thoughts and prayers after a racialized terror event, we do violence in multiple ways. Because we do not experi-ence the harmful, even fatal, consequences of racism, our words without tangible change reflect our lack of understanding and empathy for the depth of the pain and trauma effected by such events. Because of white segregation, "thoughts and prayers" reveals our unwillingness to avail ourselves of the abundant information about the realities of racism and responses that don't trivialize the depth of the harm it (and other super-ficial responses) perpetrates. Finally, but not exhaustively, when those of us who are white respond to racial terror and trauma with our "thoughts and prayers," we center our own comfort level and timeline for creating and protecting REAL racial justice and equity.

For those of us who are white who want to do anti-racism work, we must in all places and at all times override our lifelong training to protect our stake in the system of racism by staying silent. We must interrogate, not simply reflect upon, the ways in which our silence has been protective cover for our commitments to racism over and above the well-being, safe-ty, survival, health, and thriving of Black, Indigenous, Pacific-Islander, Asian, and Latino/x people. We must take stock of how our silence has perpetrated the same, different, and intensifying violence against people with whom we have dishonestly proclaimed our friendship, partnership, and alliance. (Yes, I said dishonestly. REAL TALK.)

REAL TALK means we must never look away from the violent realities of our silence or the stark language that exposes our deep commitments to allowing the system of racism to continue to benefit us over our procla-mations of anti-racist intentions. REAL TALK means those of us who are white must continue anti-racism work with equal dual focus on internal work that exorcises our demonic commitment to benefit at the expense of BIPAL people, and external work that interrupts racism in every single ex-pression. However, REAL TALK must also include dismantling how white people reinvent our racism by co-opting anti-racism strategies with racist acts that are coded in church talk.

It should be clear for all of us who are white that we cannot stay silent in the face of racism while also proclaiming (and even pretending) to do anti-racism work. And yet, white people have co-opted the anti-racism strategy of "silence is violence" and insidiously cloaked it in the liturgical practice of prayer. It might be easy enough for all of us to recognize racism when it shows up in the content of prayer: language, stereotypes, prejudices. But REAL TALK: Would you be surprised to learn that even the *very act* of prayer can be racist?

I remember the first time I recognized the act of prayer as racist. I was cofacilitating a workshop for a general agency of a white-dominant Christian Protestant denomination, and a recent racialized terror event was brought into the conversation. As details of the event were described, the weight of the room became palpable. Words were offered less and less as a deep sorrow and lament filled the space. Simultaneously, the white people in the room became visibly uncomfortable. It was not until a white person interrupted the silence with a demand to enter into prayer that I realized the stark nature of how even the act of prayer can be racist. The white person stood up and proclaimed, with the confidence of someone who expected to be listened to (and obeyed), that we needed to stop everything and go into prayer before God. That we all needed God's grace to heal us from the sin of racism and to bring racial reconciliation and justice to our world.

Perhaps because I was new in my tenure in that position and had spent the last six years training for ordination and serving in ministry in the AME Church, I was shocked when the silent, aching lament of the BIPAL people who were in the room was disrupted by an act pretending to be holy. I had become accustomed to the sacred need for people to have the space and time to have silence to honor the lament that has no words—especially after racialized terror events. I was jolted out of my assumptions with a literal demand for prayer—one that centered the comfort of those of us in the room who were white during a time when our focus should have been on attending to the needs of those directly targeted by the racism and the trauma that resulted.

REAL TALK: Every single anti-racism strategy, even something as central as "silence is violence," can be and is co-opted by white people to perpetrate and protect our racism. Thus, the disrupting and dismantling of racism must attend simultaneously to the violence of racism, the violence of silence—especially that of white silence—and the violence of racism that emerges from racist mimicry of anti-racism strategies themselves. Those of us who are white must refuse to stay silent, yes, but we must also refuse to coerce God to enact racial justice in ways that erase our responsibility for it.

ACTION-NOW Learning Engagement: The Horizon of Silence

The Horizon of Silence

Holy Silence	Silence of Learning	Protective Silence	Thoughts & Prayers	Silence Language	Repressive Silence
The deepest honoring of a person's wholeness	Silence for learning anti-racism & unlearning racism	Protects one's self from the risks of racism or responsibilites of anti racism	Empty phrases and inactive plattitudes that perpetuate racism	Omission of words, phrases, and language	Overtalking that insists white voices, values, and standards are litmus tests for normalcy

This chapter has focused on REAL TALK and how "silence is violence" is used as an anti-racism strategy and simultaneously co-opted to perpetrate racism. This ACTION-NOW Learning Engagement utilizes what we're calling the Horizon of Silence to help identify how we can engage in REAL TALK in three steps and then three more. The diagram reflects a range of expressions of silence, from that which promotes anti-racism to that which protects racism. Each includes a brief description, an example, and several racially positioned action items you can utilize right now. Remembering that anti-racism work requires concrete actions that disrupt, dislodge, and dismantle racism, make your own commitment schedule to enact these REAL STRATEGIES in REAL TIME for REAL CHANGE.

HOLY SILENCE

Description: The silence that holds space and time for the deep and sacred work of lament, grief, discernment, and truth-telling. The enactment of holding silence for the work of anti-racism to occur. Here, *holy* includes both aspects of a faith-life and what it means to be deeply human. Rather than strictly a religious phrase, "holy silence" refers to the deepest honoring of a person's wholeness.

Example: Holding silence to create holy space for BIPAL people to share their testimonies of harm.

A BIPAL person shares their testimony of harm based in their experience of being a direct target of racism. Others, including both BIPAL and white folks protect the space by keeping silent and refusing the temptation to interrupt silence, even with prayer.

ACTION-NOW Learning Engagements:

For Black, Indigenous, Pacific-Islander, Asian, and Latino/x People:

- Implement an act of resistance when someone else interrupts holy silence. Be direct in expressing the need for centering BIPAL people to express our lament and grief in the aftermath of racialized terror. For example, call it out by saying to white people, "Practice decentering yourself by remaining silent" OR by saying to yourself or other BIPAL folks, "We have a right to center our needs and to lament our grief in holy silence."

For white people:

- Refuse to replace concrete anti-racism actions with "thoughts and prayers" statements and services. Research responsible ways to respond to racialized terror and trauma as directed by BIPAL authors and activists. Pay for learning by supporting artists and activists through Patreon (or through other platforms that support them), purchasing published works, or hiring BIPAL speakers and trainers.

For Anyone:

- Practice resisting the temptation to interrupt lament or testimonies with calls for reconciliation or religious liturgies, including prayers. Make note of specific times when you are most tempted to interrupt holy silence. Name at least one phrase you will say to yourself to remind you of the importance of holding holy silence.

SILENCE OF LEARNING

Description: The silence necessary for the learning of new information and anti-racism strategies, and for the unlearning of the logic and expressions of racism.

Example: White people listening more to learn how to recognize racism in REAL TIME faster.

White people who are becoming more aware of the prevalence of racism, but who are still asking questions about specific examples or how to respond, should speak less and listen more. REAL TALK.

ACTION-NOW Learning Engagements:

For Black, Indigenous, Pacific-Islander, Asian, and Latino/x People:

- Believe other BIPAL folks when they express their experiences of racism. Interrogate our responses to ensure they are not expressing ideologies and stereotypes stemming from internalized racism. Research and practice collaboration models of anti-racism among BIPAL people instead of using zero-sum models that reinforce racism and have BIPAL people fighting against each other.

For white people:

- Believe Black, Indigenous, Pacific-Islander, Asian, and Latino/x people when they express their experiences of racism and enact strategies they create or cosign as effective and meaningful. Interrogate any initial, even brief, responses of disbelief of BIPAL people's testimonies. Include also critical assessment of any of our immediate statements to defend our anti-racism including, "Oh, but I do believe BIPAL people."

- Name specifically how the anti-racism work you are doing right now actually has been directly influenced by or directed by a BIPAL testimony or strategy. Practice doing that.

For Anyone:

- Remember that we all have something more to learn. Practice paying attention to times when we need most to learn in silence. Take our racial positionality seriously by refusing to enact learning silence to shrink ourselves for white comfort (this is for BIPAL people), or to reenact the white supremacy that overvalues white people's wisdom and logic (this is for white folks).

PROTECTIVE SILENCE

Description: The silence that protects oneself from risks of racism or the responsibilities of anti-racism.

Example: White people remaining <u>silent in</u> order to protect themselves from losing status, reputation, position, or benefits.

A white person who has attended anti-racism workshops outlining scripted interruptions of racism allows a racist comment to occur in a meeting by their boss because they are afraid of losing their job and/or social status.

ACTION-NOW Learning Engagements:

<u>For Black, Indigenous, Pacific-Islander, Asian, and Latino/x People:</u>

- Here, protective silence is a little different. The same strategies enacted by white people that perpetrate racism can sometimes be used by us to enact anti-racism. The focus is on our survival. For example, we might remain silent when our rights are being violated by a police officer to at least give ourselves a chance to survive the encounter.

<u>For white people:</u>

- Learn and practice scripts for interrupting racism in REAL TIME rather than relying on BIPAL people to do so. For example, when a white person interrupts a BIPAL person, look at the white person and say, "Excuse me." Then, look at the BIPAL person and ask, "Would you like to continue?" or "Did you have more to say?"

THOUGHTS AND PRAYERS

Description: The silence that reduces responses to empty phrases and inactive platitudes that perpetrate racism with more talk instead of encouraging the REAL TALK of anti-racism.

Example: A popular church leader offers their thoughts and prayers on a Facebook post after the latest police-enacted racialized murder.

A church pastor with a wide-reaching audience of both BIPAL and white people posts the following: "Offering our thoughts and prayers to the families of both the police officer and the victim during these trying times."

ACTION-NOW Learning Engagements:

For Black, Indigenous, Pacific-Islander, Asian, and Latino/x People:

- Stop submitting to the guilt of being the only group required to offer grace when justice is denied. Refuse to reduce acts of anti-racist resistance to prayers that remove our responsibility to be agents of REAL CHANGE in REAL TIME.

For white people:

- Never use the phrase *thoughts and prayers* as a response to racialized terror, because the phrase holds no anti-racism weight. Instead, call out the racism directly and stand with the BIPAL people directly impacted by following their lead and obeying their anti-racism strategies. Interrogate any resistance you have to the phrase *obeying their anti-racism strategies*. REAL TALK.

For Anyone:

- Refuse to create false equivalencies between the victim(s) and perpetrator(s) of racialized terror. Name specifically the responsibilities of the perpetrator to be accountable for their racism. Interrogate your need for more proof regarding who the true perpetrator is, and the racism that upholds that need. Refuse any "both sides" arguments.

SILENCE LANGUAGE

Description: The silence assumed and enforced by the omission of words, phrases, and language that will change policies, practices, and standards from racist to anti-racist.

Example: A promotion board uses the word *effective* to evaluate managerial candidates' potential.

Although all evaluation committees have criteria for selection and training, when words like *effective, transformative leader*, and *culture fit* are used without specific definitions, all the racialized implicit bias, stereotypes, and prejudices present in the evaluation and evaluators are embedded within the evaluation standards that emerge from them.

ACTION-NOW Learning Engagements:

For Black, Indigenous, Pacific-Islander, Asian, and Latino/x People:

- Review all legal, procedural, and best practices language and policies.

- Identify the language that silences and omits the factors of systemic racism that create and sustain racial inequities.

- Remember and internalize the words of Ms. Audre Lorde, who shared her daughter's Sankofa wisdom that "you're never really a whole person if you remain silent, because there's always that one little piece inside you that wants to be spoken out, and if you keep ignoring it, it gets madder and madder and hotter and hotter, and if you don't speak it out, one day it will just up and punch you in the mouth from the inside."[11]

- Create language that exposes the specific ways in which underlying systemic racism negatively and unequally burdens and harms BIPAL people and organizations.

For white people:

- Unlearn the word *share* when redistributing money from white organizations who have more capital and resources than BIPAL organizations. Remember the phrase "You can't share what you steal" and practice teaching other white people the specifics of how

---

[11] Audre Lorde, "The Transformation of Silence into Language and Action," in *Sister Outsider: Essays & Speeches by Audre Lorde* (Berkeley: Crossing Press, 2007), 42.

white supremacy and racism created an overabundance in white organizations to the detriment of BIPAL-led organizations.

- Begin immediately using the term and enforcing the policies of racial equity instead of racial equality. Equality cannot be reached using measures of equality—adding the same amount to unequal starting points continues inequality. Equity recognizes and confronts historic, present, and compounding inequality, and it tries with concrete measures to address it.

For Anyone: (for example, BMCR's open letter, 2020)[12]

- Look for and challenge all language (workplace, theological, legal, and so on) that prioritizes order instead of racial justice.

- Refuse to be distracted by strategy conversations that focus on the symptoms of racism instead of the structural racism that undergirds them.

- Unlearn the word forgive for debt incurred based in white supremacist policies and practices. Learn to use the word reparations to expose racialized inequities that have caused economic harm and that need to be redressed by concrete economic redistribution.

---

[12] Sheila Beckford, Tiffany French-Goffe, Richard Hayes, Dorlimar Lebron Malavé and Laurel Scott, "Open Letter to Bishop Bickerton," Black Methodists for Church Renewal NYAC, Google form, published July 30, 2020, https://docs.google.com/forms/d/e/1FAIpQLSflQM-L5L95LWs3zw5m2CRSSfqxPJKkIINSPQ1bbQWaGSwjyLQ/viewform.

REPRESSIVE SILENCE

Description: The silence that restricts the ideologies, voices, and REAL anti-racism STRATEGIES of BIPAL people in order to uphold white supremacy. In layman's terms: overtalking that insists that white voices, values, and standards are the litmus test for normalcy.

Example: An organization (even a social justice organization) uses BIPAL "diversity hires" without organizational change.

An organization's hiring process includes a nondiscrimination statement, it boasts a diversity and inclusion coordinator, and 5 percent of their workforce are Employees of Color, including one middle manager. The grooming policy in the HR handbook states that "hair should be clean, combed, and neatly trimmed or arranged."

ACTION-NOW Learning Engagements:

For Black, Indigenous, Pacific-Islander, Asian, and Latino/x People:

- Challenge policies that pressure BIPAL people to conform to and internalize beauty standards of whiteness that uphold racism. For example, respond to discriminatory grooming policies by referencing the CROWN Act (or the Creating a Respectful and Open World for Natural Hair Act of 2020) passed in California, New York, New Jersey, and Virginia, which "prevents employers from creating and enforcing grooming policies that they say are race neutral but really affect protected classes negatively and unequally."[13]

For white people:

- Name at least four (4) ways the description of the company example above indicates policies or language that upholds white supremacy and racism. Do additional research if necessary, ensuring you are listening to BIPAL voices.

- Require your organization to hire an external BIPAL-owned company to complete a racial equity audit for all policies, practices, and procedures. Utilize and be unflinchingly willing to risk positional and social capital to do so.

---

[13] "Hair and Grooming Discrimination," WorkplaceFairness.org, accessed January 1, 2021.

<u>For Anyone:</u>

- Work to create an anti-racist environment by naming and changing any policy or best practices list that demands repressive silence.
- Disrupt white overtalking.

Chapter 3:

REAL STRATEGIES

REAL STRATEGIES prioritizes ACTION-NOW Learning Engagements to move everyone beyond just talking about racism to immediate anti-racism actions. ACTION-NOW Learning Engagements are exercises that bridge the gap between learning about something and doing something. Rather than relying on models that demand that talk (REAL or otherwise) occur first and in isolation from action, REAL STRATEGIES places action at the center of Anti-Racism 4REALS. If anti-racism is anything that *actually* interrupts and dismantles racism, it just makes sense that actions are necessary. However, so much of current anti-racism practice, including that within the Church, is predicated on talking about and agreeing on truth of content, strategies necessary, and actions in order to engage. REAL STRATEGIES breaks the chains of information-only workshops—even at the introductory entry point—by creating processes by which action can be taken right now to dislodge, disrupt, and dismantle racism. Without real strategies, even the realest of real talk becomes just more talk. REAL STRATEGIES make REAL TALK real.

REV. LEDDER'S RESPONSE: During my time as an anti-racism trainer, I've come to realize that workshop hoarding is a real thing. Among those of us who are white, *gathering knowledge about* racism can actually become a substitute for *doing the work of* anti-racism. After racialized terror events, white organizations—including churches and social justice non-profits—flood the emails and call logs of anti-racism groups begging* to schedule training sessions on white privilege, anti-racism, or implicit bias. With newly amplified shame or guilt or awareness, white people engage in a form of educational pornography—taking what we desire (information) without any of the responsibility for the work it takes to develop anything substantive (anti-racism change).

*Begging

Actually, REAL TALK: In both literal and symbolic ways, white people and white-dominant organizations demand anti-racism training, especially after a racialized terror event. For example, after the murder of Mr. George Floyd in 2020, I received emails with attached sermons from white preachers telling me to correct their sermon for anti-racism with a timeline attached, or providing one date (with a short timeline) for when they wanted to schedule a workshop, or telling me that I should adjust the content and tone of what I say in order to ensure that their white constituents would feel "invited into the work." Even in their heightened awareness of the need to do anti-racism work, the way they reached out for "help" to dismantle racism reinforced the white entitlement taught to us by white supremacy. More disturbing, were the disgusting displays of entitlement spewed at BIPAL people doing this work. Patronizing, whitesplaining, coercing language that expected BIPAL people—especially Black women doing justice work—to bend to white leaders' wishes, superficially coded in "we need to learn more." No mention of or space given to process racialized terror events preceded even the most "progressive" of white leaders' and pastors' false equivalencies between BIPAL people's pain and the need for those of us who are white to gain awareness and do the work of anti-racism. "Begging?" Nope—straight-up racism without a shred of shame or humanity.

4REALS uses REAL STRATEGIES to get people into the work of anti-racism with the least amount of cushion and the fewest excuses to get out of it. Even the name of the exercises we use, ACTION-NOW Learning Engagements, has been crafted to highlight the urgency of the work and the immediacy of options.

In a very real way, REAL STRATEGIES provide entry points for every single person to have REAL options for doing the work of anti-racism as soon as they read the chapter, leave the workshop, or click "leave meeting." By using entry points instead of journey language, we eliminate all concern or any excuses that not all people are ready to do the work of anti-racism right now. This doesn't mean in any way, however, that some people will still not do the work of anti-racism. But that is a choice that REAL STRAT-

EGIES brings to the surface. The reality that every single white person can do anti-racism work right now presents an opportunity for rationalizations against us doing so to rise to the surface for assessment and critique. Words like "Well, I would, but ..." or "I don't understand how ...", or any of the plethora of excuses those of us who are white have been allowed to get away with, hold no weight when options for the immediate are presented. For those of us who are white, our anti-racism work must necessarily dislodge, disrupt, and dismantle all excuses for not doing whatever it takes to eradicate racism in all of its forms every single time it shows up.

INTERNAL ASSESSMENT: Write here your first thoughts after reading the sentence below.

> *For those of us who are white,*
> ***every single one of our excuses***
> *for not doing the work of anti-racism right now*
> ***is racist.***

One way REAL STRATEGIES helps to do the work of anti-racism is by removing the justifications racism has taught us to use to delay or refuse to do the work. Some of these justifications include saying that it's ok for us to wait, that we need to do more research first, or that we need to be "ready" to get started.

(Not Even Close to the Full List of) Excuses White People Use to Avoid Doing Anti-Racism Work Now

<u>White folks</u>: *Check off all the excuses you have used and write below each checkmark what action you will take the next time this excuse comes up for you.*

<u>BIPAL people</u>: *Check all excuses you have heard white people use and write below each checkmark what action you will take (or not take) the next time this excuse comes up in front of you.*

☐ The rate of loans/my history with my bank/the complicated nature of accounts with my bank is such that transferring my money/accounts/loans/mortgage to a Black-owned bank wouldn't be "smart" at this time.

☐ You have to understand, my family is just "that way." They don't know any better; they grew up in a different time; they don't mean anything by it; they're stuck in their ways; this is my family/heritage/blood; or they're going to take time to change.

☐ I'm just one person in a huge or complex organization (church, denomination, university, society, corporation—nothing I do will make a difference.

☐ I have to hold on to my character and values even as I do anti-racism work, so I will not sacrifice being polite/civil/courteous/nice/good when confronting racism or people.

☐ I agree with the message but not the tactics.

The exercise above serves (at least) a dual purpose. First, it provides a list of common excuses (and types of excuses) used to get out of doing anti-racism work by those of us who are white. When white folks see this list, it not only challenges us to name specifically the excuses we use, it also makes our brains acutely aware of when they show up in the future. You know how after you buy a red car you all of a sudden see a bunch of red cars on the road? It's not because there was a boom in red car sales. It's because your brain has been primed to see them. Same thing here.[14]

Second, the exercise above confronts those of us who are white with the specific task of determining ahead of time what we will do instead. Here, we may have already learned from our reading, from workshops, or from BIPAL people directly what actions are necessary to counter our racism. However, often we have ignored the vast knowledge available and discredited the BIPAL people who write, share, and present it, because of the way white segregation and white supremacy work, respectively. Thus, at this point it may be necessary to do the work required to learn what to do and how to do it. This is part of our work as white folks—and we can't disrupt, dislodge, and dismantle racism without it.

Rev. Ledder's REAL TALK: Just because I write about anti-racism and deeply believe that those of us who are white must enact anti-racism strategies without excuse doesn't mean there is any way I can get from my own whiteness to anti-racism work without intervention. In other words, I have had to learn directly and indirectly from BIPAL people what strategies are needed to disrupt, dislodge, and dismantle racism. I didn't wake up one day and figure out anti-racism. It is impossible for me, as a white person, to create ex nihilo any of these strategies without first learning the strategies BIPAL people have created. Additionally, even after learning about REAL STRATEGIES, the reality is that I don't always implement them at all, implement them correctly, or implement them without sweat rolling down my back as I do. White supremacy has taught me to protect my unearned racialized privileges and benefits by keeping quiet, by staying out of it, and by ignoring my responsibility to dismantle racism wherever and whenever it shows up. I must commit without reserve to do this work no matter how I feel or how I fail. REAL STRATEGIES

---

[14] The Reverend E. Michelle Ledder first used this example when writing a workbook called *Implicit Bias: What We Don't Think We Think* during her time at the General Commission on Religion and Race (GCORR) of the United Methodist Church.

don't become REAL without implementation—and implementation only becomes REAL with accountability (more in the **REAL CHANGE** chapter).

It might seem as if this is the perfect segue into anti-racism to-do and not-to-do lists. And please believe that they are coming. However, we'll first pull back the pedagogical veil to reveal the art and science of anti-racism teaching. By looking at anti-racism to-do and not-to-do lists *as a strategy* (before looking at what they actually say to do or not to do), those of us who are white can be better prepared to avoid the racism we enact when we do the "right thing" in the wrong way. By considering how to-do and not-to-do anti-racism lists are constructed, white folks can reduce the racism we perpetrate via appropriation, white saviorism, and white supremacy.

Anti-racism to-do and not-to-do lists are a strategy in and of themselves. I want to be clear—I am not damning to-do and not-to-do lists. They're a great place to start when people are just learning about a subject or just beginning the actions of putting learning into place. When created and followed honorably, anti-racism to-do and not-to-do lists can bring the "more talk" pseudo-anti-racism into the work of dislodging, disrupting, and dismantling racism. When asked by white folks where to start—or when white folks say they don't know where to start—I often tell them to do a critical Google search for "ten things we wish white allies would do" and "ten things we wish white allies would stop doing" lists written by BIPAL people—and for such a time as this, by Black people specifically.

What this *does not mean*, though, is that white folks can begin critiquing these lists or the BIPAL people who wrote them. Rather, when those of us who are white first start out, we have little to no experience with discerning whether a particular strategy is honorable for us to engage in. Thus, a critical search in this context means to find three to five lists in each category (again, written by BIPAL people generally, and right now Black people specifically) and look for the overlap. Then start doing those things. BIPAL people do not think, act, live, write, suggest, protest, resist, invite, struggle, demand, challenge, strategize, or anything else as a monolith. It is impossible to find one anti-racism to-do or not-to-do list that will encapsulate everything BIPAL folks advise white people to do or not do to fight against racism. However, by starting with the overlap, those of us who are white can be primed to do the least amount of damage and perpetrate the least amount of racism while following the to-do or not-to-do anti-racism lists.

WRITE YOUR RESPONSES BELOW: *Did it shock you that we said "least amount of damage and racism" instead of "the greatest amount of good?" Why or why not? How does this refine your anti-racism work?*

Having a starting point or even a finely curated anti-racism to-do or not-to do list doesn't eliminate the possibility that those of us who are white will perpetrate racism while using them. Here, it is most likely that white folks who identify ourselves as liberal or progressive will use these lists in ways that enact the expressions of racism for which we are most known (page ##). There are many entry points for dismantling these expressions of ally-list racism, but one to start with is the one from the 4REALS introduction: racial positionality.

If you recall, racial positionality says that because we live in a racialized society, and because society has different rules, treatment, benefits, protections, and punishments depending on our racial identities, we experience the world—and the world experiences us—differently based on race. When we start hearing "We all have different work to do" regarding anti-racism, this is where that starts. We have different risks, responsibilities, and work because of where we are positioned within the system of racism. White folks have been shoving our work onto the backs of BIPAL people this whole time, which is why the system and its expressions still exist and why BIPAL people have been fighting and resisting it their whole lives. Because BIPAL people are the direct targets of racism, they are the most capable of determining strategies or lists with anti-racist outcomes and which kinds of work white people should implement.

> *Interrupting white people's racism*
> *is always the work of white people.*
> *No matter what BIPAL people decide are*
> *their strategies,*
> *we remain steadfast knowing it is always*
> *part of our work, no matter what.*

Even within the same category of anti-racism work, the work of white people and the work of BIPAL people are often different. Addressing and dealing with white manipulation (fragility) is a perfect example with which we should start. *White fragility* is a term often used in anti-racism work and heard more frequently since white sociologist Robin DiAngelo got the term published in her book of the same name. Although it is a phenomenon recognized and resisted by BIPAL people for as long as racism has existed, DiAngelo often receives unmitigated citation credit misinformed by white privilege and supremacy. A paraphrase of the published term's definition describes the symbolic but very real line, in conversations about racism or work to dismantle it, that when crossed makes white people so uncomfortable that we engage in a set of predictable acts or reactions, including but not limited to pouting, silence, shutting down, crying, anger, defense, and walking out.

When groups that include white people ask for anti-racism training and have a needs list that rivals the eternal length of pi, or the limit that they can only "do one training for now," I usually recommend a workshop on white manipulation (fragility). When white folks are involved, whether we are dominant in numbers or entitlement, white manipulation (fragility) will obstruct even the best anti-racism strategies. White manipulation (fragility) is the weaponization of whiteness and of humanness for the sake of whiteness. Left unchecked, it creates a power vortex that sucks up all the attention and energy that should be focused on race, racism, and anti-racism and coerces it to care for and protect white people. Emotions and responses of discomfort are not bad in and of themselves. However, when these are used as weapons to manipulate energy and people in order to coddle the very ones responsible for the racism, they are racist.

And here's where racial positionality comes back into play. It's not just that white people enact white manipulation (fragility) and thus are responsible for it—though we do and we are. It's that to dismantle white manipulation (fragility), we must engage in different strategies based on our racial identity. White people must build our *resilience* to white manipulation (fragility). Those of us who are white must resist the temptation to weaponize our emotions, reactions, and whiteness to get away with our racism and away from our responsibility for it. To do so, we build up our *resilience* to the reactionary responses we have relied upon to alleviate our guilt and shame. All resilience against our white manipulation (fragility) is built for the purpose of doing more and more anti-racism work before our white manipulation (fragility) kicks up again. White people must, at all times, refuse to demand care from BIPAL people or minimize our responsibility for our own racism and white manipulation (fragility). We must work to dislodge, disrupt, and dismantle our racism without putting that burden on our BIPAL siblings.

REV. BECKFORD'S RESPONSE: Just recently I purchased a set of fabric resistance bands for strengthening purposes. I underwent a procedure some years ago that left me with a limited range of motion. I first used bands made of rubber to achieve the same purpose; however, the rubber bands rolled up and I would have to pause my workout to fix them. After learning about the fabric resistance bands, I did my research, then made a purchase.

I used the first-level fabric band for a few days. It was a bit of a struggle until I got into a groove. I found that as I continued to use the band, my routine became easier, even though as I stretched the band the resistance increased. I used the first-level band for a time before realizing that the band had done its job. I had achieved a level of strength, but I could not progress if I continued using the same level. I moved up to the next level of resistance represented by a different color. I began with pink, then moved to gray as my leg muscles *were conditioned* to the first level of resistance.

BIPAL people have been taught via "the talk," oral stories, historical facts, and our present reality through racialized terror to be resilient, but resistance is something we must build up. Philip Spencer Lake's comparison between resilience and resistance is helpful here: "The capacity to weather a disturbance without loss is defined as resistance, whereas resilience is the capacity to recover from a disturbance after incurring losses." In other words, resilience requires loss, while resistance prevents loss.[15]

We, BIPAL people, have got to do better in building resistance to white supremacy and racism. Knowing the stories and conjuring up the resistance our ancestors had will help. Since the killing of Mr. George Floyd, I have noticed many of our people posting the most disrespectful meme that dishonors the strength, tenacity, resilience, resistance, and "stick-to-itiveness" of our ancestors.

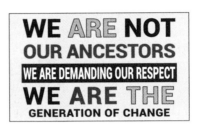

This meme replicates the lies of the whitewashed history retold by conditioned BIPAL people that our ancestors were not the authors of change but simply submissive to the whims and wills of white people. Yet, it is only because of their determination to resist dehumanization that we are even here to continue the demands for respect, liberation, justice, and equity and the command to "keep your knee off of our necks!"

- Whitewashed history will make you think the Reverend Dr. Martin Luther King Jr. was the most beloved "Negro" at the time of his life and death, but actually, research tells us that he had a 75 percent approval rating in 1968.[16]
- Whitewashed history will make you believe that Rosa Parks refused to give up her seat because the Civil Rights Movement was a movement for all people, as taught to my child by her white elementary school teacher.

[15] Philip S. Lake, "Resistance, Resilience and Restoration," *Ecological Management & Restoration* 14, no. 1, (2012): 20, https://doi.org/10.1111/emr.12016.

[16] James C. Cobb, "Even Though He Is Revered Today, MLK Was Widely Disliked by the American Public When He Was Killed," *Smithsonian Magazine* (April 4, 2018), https://www.smithsonianmag.com/history/why-martin-luther-king-had-75-percent-disapproval-rating-year-he-died-180968664/.

- Whitewashed history will make you believe that the war on drugs was not a strategy to incarcerate BIPAL people, mainly Black and Latino/x people.[17]
- Whitewashed history told by conditioned BIPAL people would make you believe that slaves were immigrants.[18]

These fallacies of whitewashed history are not just history. Legacies of pulling yourself up by your bootstraps are repeated today without factoring in the long history of oppressive systems such as redlining, racially discriminatory hiring, white flight, the underfunding of educational institutions, and the overfunding of the prison industrial complex.

BIPAL people have become conditioned to accept and expect racism. Some of us continue to use the beginning level of resistance until our anti-racism muscles atrophy. As our muscles continue to weaken even as we mimic the movements of resistance, our best efforts can no longer disrupt, dislodge, and dismantle racism. We must be like our ancestors, whose strategies of resistance included the following:

- Not laziness but intentional "slowdowns"
- Not passive aggressiveness but premeditated and calculated action plans
- Not submission to white supremacy but tactical measures used to select leadership of their choosing
- Not nonthreating BIPAL leadership that earned the approval of white people or a white system, but audacious leadership that defies and rejects whiteness as "truth" and normalcy

Internalized oppression turns BIPAL people against BIPAL people while we do the bidding of white supremacy.

---

[17] Michelle Alexander, *The New Jim Crow: Mass Incarceration in the Age of Colorblindness* (New York: New Press, 2010).

[18] Liam Stack, "Ben Carson Calls Slaves 'Immigrants' in First HUD Remarks," *The New York Times* (March 6, 2017), https://www.nytimes.com/2017/03/06/us/politics/ben-carson-refers-to-slaves-as-immigrants-in-first-remarks-to-hud-staff.html.

For BIPAL people only: Share a time when you either witnessed, participated in, or urged an action that perpetrated racialized harm against your BIPAL sibling: **White people, DO NOT RESPOND!**

_____

_____

_____

_____

_____

For white people: Knowing that the previous question is off-limits to you, interrogate your reaction to the instruction "DO NOT RESPOND!"

_____

_____

_____

_____

_____

Resistance to whiteness as normalcy is imperative to anti-racism work. BIPAL people must identify (interrogate) the lure of provocative means of advancement that forces us to denounce our thoughts, ideas, history, and ancestral teachings and accept whiteness—white thoughts, white value systems, white religion, and white mediocrity—as a measure of success. Resistance must decenter whiteness. One REAL STRATEGY to decenter whiteness calls for us to cease coddling white people's manipulation (fragility).

White people's manipulation (fragility) is usually coded as an "attack" on the white person. When white people use the term "attack" to describe being confronted with their racism, this is a tactic to take the focus off of the racism and recenter whiteness. It is also a signal for other white people to join in, and it elicits sympathy or coddling from BIPAL people. What I mean by coddling white manipulation (fragility) is coming to the white person's rescue, making the offending white person feel as if they are more important than the offended BIPAL person, and allowing white manipulation (fragility) to recenter whiteness when the concern should be focused on dislodging, disrupting, and dismantling racism.

For BIPAL people: How often have you witnessed or participated in coddling white people's manipulation (fragility)? Please check all that apply to you; then explain.

- ☐ They don't know any better
- ☐ They did not mean it that way
- ☐ I know their heart
- ☐ You are making this about race when they are hurting
- ☐ Can we stop and pray?
- ☐ What they mean by this is
- ☐ They are trying, give them credit
- ☐ They didn't grow up around BIPAL people, so they don't know
- ☐ We need to say it in a way that does not offend
- ☐ They feel attacked
- ☐ This doesn't bring unity

For white people: How many of these have been used on your behalf or used specifically by you to protect your own white manipulation (fragility) or that of another white person? Please check all that apply. In the lines below, explain how these actually perpetrate racism.

- ☐ I feel attacked
- ☐ I didn't know that was racist

☐ I never had BIPAL friends growing up

☐ I didn't mean that

☐ I would never hurt anyone

☐ My feelings are hurt

☐ More tears

☐ You don't understand

☐ Why are you making this about race/not everything is about race

☐ I'm not like them/other white folk (Yes, this is white manipulation [fragility])

☐ I've marched in many protests

☐ I have a Black Lives Matter sign on my lawn

The reality of white manipulation (fragility) is not new to BIPAL people. White tears, defending, deflecting, and making a conflict about hurt feelings is a strategy that white people use to distance themselves from the evils of their racism.

White people's manipulation (fragility) also influences who BIPAL people select to lead in our own communities. If a BIPAL person is too loud or too outspoken in our own communities, we determine that that particular person with those characteristics could not lead because "no one" (meaning white folk) will follow them. BIPAL leaders shun them, try to tell them to tone it down, or make disparaging remarks about them. In most cases, BIPAL people's primary goal is not to hinder each other's growth. This is not the crabs-in-a-barrel mentality that we often hear about. It is coddling whiteness to the detriment of our own advancement.

> *The crabs-in-a-barrel mentality: Crabs are thrown in a wooden barrel. As one advances to the top, another crab grabs its leg to attempt its own escape. However, the outcome prevents both crabs from getting out. I always ask, "Who made the barrel? What was its purpose? Who put the crabs in the barrel?"*

I recall having a loud disagreement with a man outside. An older Black woman approached me without knowing the events leading up to the argument and said, "A lady doesn't carry herself that way; Black women must be quiet but strong. That's how we survived [slavery]." After returning home and sharing these events with my mother, she said, "Served him right! A lady knows how to be ready to defend herself." With that one statement, my mother shut some doors inside of me and opened another. From that day forward, hearing those words and the message of liberation that they instilled in me, I vowed to be my own definition of a lady and no one else's. That moment formed me and breathed into me a new understanding of the responsibility of resisting "respectability politics" and defying the effects of white supremacy no matter from whom they come.

> *We are trained to be what whiteness determines us to be. We are conditioned to accept leaders who will conform to whiteness. Anti-racist REAL STRATEGIES demand the opposite.*

White people understand racial positionality well. They have used it in their playbook to further their agenda to create structures that allow them to remain in power and to divide BIPAL people as a tactic. Plays found there begin with positioning BIPAL people in desirable places of authority to use us for optics. Once we're there, they pressure us to challenge anti-racist legislation that would provide for equity, accountability, transparency, and other means of resistance. Historically, white people then misuse the BIPAL people's positioning to weaken BIPAL structures of resistance in order to infiltrate, control, and manipulate outcomes in favor of strengthening white supremacy through effective racist policies and structures. BIPAL people, both wittingly and unwittingly, have been engaged by white people in actions that further divide our communities.

Resistance as a REAL STRATEGY requires BIPAL people's refusal to play by any racist playbook—which first requires that we know it. Resistance for us will also include nonparticipation in any promotion, lure, or perk that results in strengthening white supremacy and dividing BIPAL communities. REAL STRATEGIES of resistance will also place a priority upon anti-racism audits of policies and procedures to ensure all racist practices are eliminated. Risk is a factor in any means of resistance, but any action of freedom or resistance is risky. We must ask ourselves, what is the alternative?

ACTION-NOW Learning Engagement

Using racial positionality, follow the REAL STRATEGY listed for your racial identity to honorably and authentically do the work of anti-racism right now.

REAL STRATEGY	BIPAL People	White People	All People
Address white manipulation (fragility)	Commit to not coming to the rescue of white people when they are confronted with their own racism and their attempts to take attention away from the offense. **Call out white manipulation (fragility); do not coddle.**	Build resilience to our own white manipulation (fragility) through the following steps: [1] Learn to manage our emotions and refuse to allow them to demand the energy and attention that should be going toward the work of anti-racism; [2] refuse to expect BIPAL people to care for us while we deal with our own guilt, shame, and awareness of our racism; and [3] refuse to defend ourselves after learning of our racism ("I didn't mean ..." or "I didn't know ..."). Rather, take the time and give the effort necessary to learn why what we did is racist and what to do instead.	Refuse to allow white manipulation (fragility) to be acceptable.

ACTION-NOW Learning Engagement

Using racial positionality, follow the REAL STRATEGY listed for your racial identity to honorably and authentically do the work of anti-racism right now.

REAL STRATEGY	BIPAL People	White People	All People
Honor BIPAL-only spaces	BIPAL people reserve the option to invite or not to invite white people. There are few spaces where BIPAL people can be themselves without judgement or the expectation to follow norms created by white people. Remember racial positionality when thinking about allowing yourself to be in a space where you have the option to invite or not to invite.	Pay close and careful attention to directions and descriptions of gathering spaces to check whether this is a BIPAL-only space. Learn and look for wording (explicit) and coding (culturally specific language) that indicates a BIPAL-only space. Learn why BIPAL-only spaces are critical and how and why white people invading them perpetrates racism and white supremacy. When (and only when) invited into a BIPAL-only space by a BIPAL person, do not speak unless asked specifically, and be especially careful to obey instructions as to what they are asking for us to do.	Do not create false equivalencies between BIPAL-only spaces and white segregated spaces.

Do not create BIPAL-only spaces as an afterthought or add-on, or in less-than-desirable/visible areas. |

ACTION-NOW Learning Engagement

Using racial positionality, follow the REAL STRATEGY listed for your racial identity to honorably and authentically do the work of anti-racism right now.

REAL STRATEGY	BIPAL People	White People	All People
Rest	Anti-racism work is extremely taxing on the bodies, minds, and spirits of BIPAL people. We can burn out while doing anti-racism work because we can never turn off our racial identity. We can try to assimilate, play respectability politics, or define ourselves by nationality to be removed from the scrutiny, harm, and racism that white supremacy thrives on, but our skin color often gives us away. White allies/accomplices can easily walk away from this work (rest). Because we are not a part of the social construction of whiteness, rest is an essential component of the resistance strategy we must create for ourselves.	A basic balance of rest and work is necessary for all human beings, but white people must also realize that feeling tired, worn out, and burned out from the work of anti-racism is part of our work. We must not create a false equivalency between our tiredness from doing work to repudiate harm that we've caused and the tiredness of BIPAL people who are experiencing harm and body/mind/spirit/soul exhaustion as part of their experience as a BIPAL person. Consider the weariness we feel a glimpse of what BIPAL people experience, and a continuous call to keep doing this work despite it.	Rest is a requirement for all human beings. Regular and balanced rest promotes the health necessary to continue to interrupt racism in REAL TIME. Burnout and self-adulatory martyrdom are not anti-racist.

ACTION-NOW Learning Engagement

Using racial positionality, follow the REAL STRATEGY listed for your racial identity to honorably and authentically do the work of anti-racism right now.

REAL STRATEGY	BIPAL People	White People	All People
BIPAL-created anti-racism strategies	Strategies that benefit BIPAL people should be created by those who are the direct targets of racism. Those who experience the harm of racism are those who know how to disrupt, dislodge, and dismantle it. Hold white allies/accomplices/people accountable for co-opting or plagiarizing the work of BIPAL people.	Follow the overarching template of anti-racism work: BIPAL people create or sign off on anti-racism strategies, white people implement the work and credit BIPAL people for it, and white people are accountable to BIPAL people for doing it correctly or faithfully. We do not appropriate the work or words or strategies of BIPAL people, recognizing that there is no pathway from our own whiteness to anti-racism work without an intervention of some sort.	Teach strategies based in racial positionality

ACTION-NOW Learning Engagement

Using racial positionality, follow the REAL STRATEGY listed for your racial identity to honorably and authentically do the work of anti-racism right now.

REAL STRATEGY	BIPAL People	White People	All People
Transfer money into institutions owned by BIPAL people	Transfer mortgages as well as business and personal accounts to Black-owned credit unions and banks. Buy Black. BIPAL people, protect your investments; invest in your communities; realize your economic power; and refuse to undervalue your worth. Place value—monetary or otherwise—on the anti-racism strategies we create and white people use.	Transfer all accounts, loans, mortgages, and credit card balances to BIPAL-owned institutions; use our social and leadership power in any organizations we are a part of to encourage others to transfer their accounts, loans, and mortgages to the same. Do not, however, transfer money into Black- or BIPAL-owned credit unions. The ownership of credit unions is determined by the accounts of the people, and thus, if enough white people transfer money into credit unions, we shift the ownership from BIPAL people to white people, furthering economic inequity.	Create economic racial equity

ACTION-NOW Learning Engagement

Using racial positionality, follow the REAL STRATEGY listed for your racial identity to honorably and authentically do the work of anti-racism right now.

REAL STRATEGY	BIPAL People	White People	All People
"Begging" / Asking for help in anti-racism work	**BIPAL PEOPLE ARE NOT OBLIGATED TO TEACH WHITE PEOPLE ABOUT RACISM.**	Interrogate whether the language (verbal or body) demands that BIPAL people help us with our anti-racism work because we've now decided it's important. Remember that it is our responsibility to obey the strategies created or cosigned by BIPAL people, but it is not their job to teach us, and even if they decide to do so, that is never on our timeline. Critically assess our language through the lens of someone who is harmed by the injustice we want to learn about. Would you recoil if an abuser asked the person they abused for "help" using the same language we use to "ask" BIPAL people for help in anti-racism work?	

ACTION-NOW Learning Engagement

Using racial positionality, follow the REAL STRATEGY listed for your racial identity to honorably and authentically do the work of anti-racism right now.

REAL STRATEGY	BIPAL People	White People	All People
Refuse to pit BIPAL people against BIPAL people	Refuse to accept the stereotype of the "crabs in a barrel" as our own reality. Resist buying into the white supremacy playbook. The playbook is to always act as if one group is speaking adversely about the other. In other words, an employer says they "would" make changes based on racial equity but can't because of competing demands from different groups of color (BIPAL people). This is a tactic used to plant seeds of discord and inevitably take the focus off of the main source of division: racism.	Learn and expose how white supremacy limits resources, access, opportunities, space, and respect for BIPAL people. Recognize how white supremacy often creates separate and unequal buckets for "everyone" and for BIPAL people—and how doing so siphons all BIPAL people to the smaller bucket to compete with each other while equating "everyone" with white folks/groups. Take a look at how BIPAL people are only offered or told about money/scholarships specifically set apart for BIPAL people but not about the money/scholarships/grants for "everyone," even though they are eligible for both.	Dismantle the zero-sum game lie. White supremacy is based in the zero-sum game, which says that if one person or group has some, there is less for everyone else. White supremacy and racism are founded on a scarcity model that keeps people and groups in competition with each other for a limited amount of resources, including but not limited to money, jobs, excellence, and even benefit of the doubt. In contrast, anti-racism highlights how oppressions and injustices create scarcity and pit people against each other. White supremacy lies to us all that white people deserve (and deserve the most) resources and must exclude all others to protect themselves.

ACTION-NOW Learning Engagement

Using racial positionality, follow the REAL STRATEGY listed for your racial identity to honorably and authentically do the work of anti-racism right now.

REAL STRATEGY	BIPAL People	White People	
Decentering White-ness	Resist recentering whiteness. Resist defending white manipulation (fragility). Resist conforming to white supremacy.	Stop saying, immediately, that we will "give up our spot" for BIPAL peoples — this defines the position as ours to give up (or "share" — this is the same thing!) — rather say, "I am stepping down, my staying reinforces and centers whiteness."	
Honor BIPAL-select-ed leadership	BIPAL people elect, affirm, and empower their own leaders. BIPAL people do not use the master's tools to dismantle the master's house.[19] Leadership is not to be selected based on criteria created by whiteness.	Obey BIPAL-selected leadership decisions and the leaders they select. Interrogate your first (and second) reaction to the word obey. Assess the racism and white supremacy behind any resistance to BIPAL-selected leadership. Refuse to use the phrase "I agree with the goal but not the tactics."	

[19] Lorde, Sister *Outsider*, 112.

Chapter 4:

REAL TIME

> Racism happens in real time, so anti-racism must also happen in REAL TIME. REAL TIME incorporates role-plays so that people can practice scripts and rehearse plans in preparation to interrupt and dismantle racism in the moment.

REAL TALK and REAL STRATEGIES can't interrupt and dismantle racism if when the racism occurs we can't enact them. But REAL TIME also addresses how racism itself obstructs the urgent necessity and the required skill sets to interrupt it. Social currency, church teachings, corporate climbing culture, and the zero-sum game are all methods that white supremacy uses to create boundaries—real and imagined—that teach us, based on our racial positionality, to obey the logic system of racism. This logic system is complete with rules and values and the ordering and timing of "proper" ways to do things. Anti-Racism 4REALS has seen how interrupting racism in REAL TIME subverts and dismantles racism because it belongs to the logic system of anti-racism.

A Few Notes Before We Get Started:

- Remember, REAL TIME means that anti-racism starts before the reading, learning, or workshop ends. Even the way we learn about anti-racism can teach anti-racism.
- Everyone is *ready* to do anti-racism. 4REALS deeply believes that to dismantle oppression is part of what it means to be human. Some people might not have the tools or resolve yet, but all people can do anti-racism work right now.
- 4REALS doesn't use journey language that tricks people into thinking the time to act comes later. Rather, we use entry points

highlighting how everyone can do something as soon as they finish the chapter, leave the workshop, or click "leave meeting."

- *We only roleplay the interruption.* When white people ask to role-play the racism so we can "recognize it," we reveal how much of our lives are steeped in white segregation, how we haven't bothered to do our own research, and how diminished our empathy must be to request a role-play of harm when it doesn't directly harm us.

REV. LEDDER'S RESPONSE: One of the most insidious and seditious phrases in the Church lexicon is "Meet the people where they are." It's meant as more than a catchphrase but has become as commonplace and overused as a bumper sticker. It's taught to pastors-in-training as an intrinsic partner to "You have to love the people." Coupled together, these imperatives—"You have to love the people" and "Meet the people where they are"—are meant to instruct pastors as to how Christian relationships ideally should work. Love, at the center of relationships, should guide our intentions and interactions. Engage in love-guided intentions and interactions, then see where people are struggling—even failing—but walk alongside them in a gentle, encouraging way toward the better, the good, and the ideal.

Imagining and hoping for pastors and churches who love each other and "meet each other where they are" provides an oasis in a world (and those "other churches") hellbent on critiquing humans into submissive obedience. The promise of love as the central value that corrects with care instead of coercing with chastisements is as alluring as it is addictive. And perhaps, if this promise is left in the idealized state and outside of anti-racism work, the world—including but not limited to the Church—would be a better place. So then, how could love and care-centered guidance be wrong?

In anti-racism work, it is clear to most that outcomes must override intentions. No matter how good the intentions are, if the outcomes create harm, there is no intention good enough to erase that harm. For example, let's say I'm presenting in a meeting at the front of the room, and someone jumps up from their seat, runs across the room toward me, and stomps on my foot as they run past me out the door. Now, in the immediacy of that we might all be looking around at each other wondering what in the world just happened. In addition, I am in searing pain and unable to stand or walk using my left foot. Three minutes later, the runner reenters the room with an ice cream cone and explains to me that he had received a text saying that mocha-chip ice cream cones were being offered in the conference room and he just couldn't get there fast enough. He says he didn't mean to step on my foot, but the lure of mocha-chip ice cream was just too powerful for him to take anything else into consideration. I immediately understand, since mocha-chip ice cream is clearly the most superior ice cream flavor of them all (prove me wrong ☺). However, this doesn't change the fact that I will need to go to the emergency room to get my foot checked out because the swelling is so bad that I won't be able to (nor should I have to) walk it off. Our relationship might be salvaged, because I understand his intention was not to harm me. But the harm has been done, must be addressed separately, and cannot be reversed with his explanation.

In anti-racism work with white people, the imperatives to "love the people" and "meet the people where they are" are corrupted in order to satisfy our need to be right, to be protected from any type of shame or guilt, and to be cared for even in the midst of our racism. "Love the people" is corrupted into an imperative to accept people's racist behavior, beliefs, and values as if love were the same thing as permission. When this happens, horrid behavior becomes equated with someone's opinion, someone's upbringing, or someone's personhood. In terms of white people and our racism, the first allows "I" statements to protect racism, the second allows "heritage" to mask harm, and the third allows abuse to imitate empathy. But true love doesn't permit oppression—it corrects it. Black activist-writer James Baldwin reminds us that love requires pointing out that which we don't currently see.[20] Dr. Cornel West proclaims that justice is what love looks like in public.[21] Love, in terms of anti-racism, then, points out racism for what it is, and corrects it until justice is made manifest.

But what does this have to do with REAL TIME? Here's where it all comes together. By combining the false sense of love with "meet the people where they are," white people are allowed to continue to perpetrate racism until, on our own timeline, we decide we are *ready* to change. When "love the people" equates to permission to continue perpetrating racism, "meet the people where they are" equates to a directive to walk alongside

---

[20] James Baldwin, "The Black Scholar Interviews James Baldwin," F. R. Standley and L. H. Pratt eds., *Conversations with James Baldwin* (Jackson: University of Mississippi Press, 1989), 142–159.

[21] Howard University Rankin Chapel, "Sermon, Cornel West," YouTube video, 26:41, April 17, 2011, https://www.youtube.com/watch?v=nGqP7S_WO6o.

the people until they give their permission for change to occur. The main problem with this, though there are many, is that our ability to choose for ourselves what we will do or not do (free will—a good thing) is conflated with our right to keep perpetrating racism (oppression). For those of us who are white, this combination is intoxicating in that it privileges our humanness/goodness, protects our affair with white supremacy, and permits our entitlement to do things on our own timeline. Although we are the ones committing evil, though we are the ones who benefit from the oppression of BIPAL people, though we are the ones at fault, we demand to feel comfort before we (and in order to) make changes. This deadly combination allows our racism in all its expressions to continue based on the timeline of the oppressor—us. In no other instance, other than from the perspective of the unrepentant oppressor, would anyone deem it fair or just that the abuser dictate the timeline of full liberation of the one(s) they abuse.

Anti-Racism 4REALS recognizes that racism must be interrupted in the moment. The momentum and compounding consequences of the expressions of racism have power beyond any single infraction. Just as an object in motion stays in motion without interference, so also does any oppression intertwined with the status quo and historic preservation. This also means that those of us who are white will use anything at our disposal as weapons with which to stave off both the need for us to change and the accountability necessary for us to do so. We are the momentum that sustains and protects racism every single time and in every single way that we obstruct the work of anti-racism—including but not limited to defiling the definition of love or mutilating what it means to be in care-filled relationship with each other. In order for white people to do the work of anti-racism, we must override our instinctual and well-honed desires to dictate the timeline by which racism will be interrupted, and instead interrupt racism in the moment every time that it occurs. As with the mocha-chip ice cream scenario, if your foot has been trampled on, then regardless of the intention or even the comfort of the abuser, your foot still needs attention. You need to get to the emergency room—and doing so shouldn't be based on the timeline of the abuser's need to finish his ice cream.

With that said, here are some scenarios in which racism occurs in everyday settings. After each scenario, I'll list some options for white folks to interrupt and dismantle racism in REAL TIME. In the ACTION-NOW

Learning Engagement for this chapter, you'll find some common expressions of racism with space for you to script your own REAL TIME scripts and responses.

Scenario 1: *During a meeting, a Black woman speaks up about the lack of diversity within the organization. After the meeting, she and many others within the same organization receive an email from a white participant stating the Black woman was volatile, hostile, and racist for constantly speaking about the need for more diverse representation within the organization.*

- If any of this language—volatile, hostile, racist—comes up during the meeting, the interruption must happen during the meeting. If it occurs only in the email, respond to the email.
- "Reply all" with your anti-racism interruption. The racism happened in public (not privately between the speaker in the meeting and the sender of the email) so the anti-racism response should be public as well. (Refer back to page 15 for an anti-racist interpretation of Matthew 18:15–17)
- The following is a possible script for your email:

  To [NAME],
  I was in the aforementioned meeting and witnessed none of the behavior descriptions you mention. Rather, Ms./Mr./Title [LAST NAME] did the organization a great service by highlighting our lack of diversity and our need for change. Furthermore, naming racism as a BIPAL person is extra work they shouldn't have to do because of the way that racism targets them. Naming the problem of racism is not racist. Your email perpetrates racism by disparaging a BIPAL person with racialized stereotypes and the charge of racism. This should be rescinded with a "reply all" apology to Ms./Mr./Title [LAST NAME] forthwith.

Scenario 2: *A Research I university created a faculty search committee comprising a Black woman professor, a white woman professor, a white male professor early in his career, and two students—a Black male student from the seminary for which the faculty search was being conducted, and a white woman PhD student from the religion department. Candidates were interviewed for the first round using Zoom. During one of the "see where we are" brainstorming sessions among the search committee, each committee member was identifying candidates to advance to the second round. The white male professor had no problem identifying each white candidate's credentials.*

When it came to assessing a Black Caribbean male candidate who had the same qualifications as one of the white male candidates, he said that he didn't think the candidate would be a good fit.

- Name what you see: "I noticed you have a much easier time naming the credentials of each of the white candidates than those of BIPAL candidates."
- Ask specifically what he means by "don't think he would be a good fit." Often times, language like this euphemizes racist statements, as in this case. Asking for specific examples of why this BIPAL candidate wouldn't be a good fit requires the white male professor to (try to) name what this euphemism is covering.
- Name the specific qualifications that the Black Caribbean candidate has in common with one of the white male candidates and ask specifically what has created the difference between the two candidates for him regarding fit.
- The more specifically you ask, the closer you will get to the racism behind the euphemism.
- In addition, point out that "not a good fit" is often used in white-dominant environments to exclude BIPAL people, BIPAL candidates for hire, or BIPAL candidates for promotion. This is a specific racist statement that should be interrupted in addition to anything else that comes from having to address the euphemism.

Scenario 3: *A group of Black people bring a grievance to the CEO of the company that spells out the inequity in distribution of funding and salaries to areas that have predominantly BIPAL people. The CEO meets with the group to listen to their ideas and calls their ideas "problematic." The CEO then rolls out the newly named "CEO Initiative" which outlines all the "problematic" ideas—now described as anti-racist—as his own, without giving the group of Black people credit.*

- Respond to the rollout in the same format in which it comes. If it is sent in an email, respond in an email. If it is introduced at a press conference, respond at the press conference. If it is presented in a ZOOM meeting, then respond during the presentation.
- As soon as the plagiarism occurs, interrupt it and name it for what it is. Name the specific items of the "CEO-named initiative" that have copied strategies and content from the document created by the group of Black people: "Excuse me, that exact strategy/wording

comes directly from the [NAME] initiative brought to you by the [NAME] group just last week. You're stealing their work and calling it anti-racism."

- Point out that the CEO identified these strategies as problematic when they came to him from Black people, but now he's using them as if they are his strategies without citing them. This is a function of white supremacy, appropriation, and entitlement. Ask in what way is he compensating the group for their ideas and strategies.
- Require an apology, the proper citing, and that compensation be made to the group, and hold CEO accountable for doing these things. Involve HR, social media, or other publicity forums if necessary.

REV. BECKFORD'S RESPONSE: In this season of calling out, calling in, and cancel culture, REAL TIME is about calling a person in—but not how you may think.

- **CALLING OUT:** The term calling out is an action step used literally to call out oppressive and appalling actions and behaviors. It has become more and more prevalent as oppressive behaviors have become increasingly publicized. Social media has made it easier to call people out—and thus call for justice. Some callouts lead to individual and institutional change—some lead to people being "cancelled."

- **CANCEL CULTURE:** Calling for boycotting businesses or some action such as resignations, firing from positions, and so on.

  Cancel culture, historically in the hands of powerful men, has been used as a tool of revenge mostly against women who have defied or denied their advances. As a deputy of anti-Blackness racism, it is also known as blackballing or blacklisting. This culture of canceling is not new to Christians. Ancient and recent history shows us we are quick to persecute those perceived to be witches, those who have a different belief system, BIPAL people, people in the LGBTQIA communities and in Jewish communities, and more. It was cancel culture that executed many BIPAL leaders, including Jesus. This tactic wielded by BIPAL people or our allies produces a different outcome. Rather than for revenge, cancel culture is used as a tool for accountability for racist and oppressive behavior.

REAL TIME ANTI-RACISM IN THE CHURCH MEETING

During a meeting at a large church conference where a group of mostly white moderates were in attendance, a prominent white pastor and author stood before the crowded room. While speaking about a group of African delegates, he said, "We invited them here to discuss the issue. We bought them pizza. The whole time we were talking to them, all they did was shake their heads. I do not know if they even understood what I was saying. I think they were just here for the pizza."

A Black woman stood up to speak about the harm that those words carried. At that point, another white facilitator stood up and asked that the conversation continue in private. The Black woman responded, "No! You said this in public; we will deal with this in public." She went on to identify the harmful words and educate those in attendance as to why the words were harmful. After she was heard, there were a number of white people who approached her and thanked her. They expressed that they knew the words were wrong, but did not know what to say to confront the racism.

For many in the field of anti-racism, *calling in* means pulling people to the side when a racial offense has happened in public. Do not "embarrass" or "challenge" the person in public, people say. Approach the offender with grace and mercy, they say. Yet, these strategies often protect the racism that anti-racism claims to dismantle. When 4REALS uses the term *calling in*, we mean that racism committed in public must be addressed in public. REAL TIME calls for the interruption of racism in the moment.

REAL TIME requires accountability and education.

(REAL TALK: Please understand that it is not the obligation of BIPAL people to educate white people on whiteness; however, we can very well call it out.)

Although many approve of the method but lack the skills to interrupt racism in REAL TIME, there are some who disapprove. This is nothing new to me or to 4REALS. While leading workshops, we encounter vehement opposition to this REAL often. One white woman responded, "You expect me to interrupt someone while they are talking in front of everyone to let them know they said something racist. Sorry, I will not be doing that! I will not embarrass anyone." Our response was to ask her which is worse: to be a BIPAL person who is devalued, dismissed, embarrassed, and denigrated while others' silence indicates acceptance of this behavior, or to stop the harm in its tracks so everyone will know it is unacceptable.

This disapproval can be found in BIPAL communities as well. I have been challenged by a Black man who shared the following: "I would have pulled him to the side instead of embarrassing him in front of others." The person that I challenged was a white Episcopal leader, so I am not sure whether the statement was made in respect to his status or for the purpose of coddling white manipulation (fragility).

For many who are Christian, the disapproval of REAL TIME interruption stems from a misinterpretation of Matthew 18:15–17, introduced on page 15. In addition, biblical references where Jesus models interrupting oppression in REAL TIME are plentiful. In Luke 13:10–17, we find Jesus healing the sick on the Sabbath. The Pharisees and the Sadducees felt responsible for calling Jesus out, prioritizing false decorum over suffering. Jesus does otherwise.

Jesus' response is not given in private. He did not say, "Oh, we'll take this up in a minute," or "Tell the woman suffering from her illness, and now even more from these dismissive statements, to wait! I want the others to feel comfortable and not attacked. I will discuss this with them in private and get back to you." *No*, her needs were at the forefront. Jesus exposes their hypocrisy and duplicity, holds them accountable, teaches everyone in earshot a lesson, and restores the woman's health and dignity in REAL TIME.

The following represent some everyday scenarios of racism. After each scenario, I've highlighted aspects of the racism perpetrated and interruptions to dismantle them.

Scenario 1: *During a meeting, a Black woman speaks up about the lack of diversity within the organization. After the meeting, she and many others within the same organization receive an email from a white participant stating the Black woman was volatile, hostile, and racist for constantly speaking about the need for more diverse representation within the organization.*

> To start off, the root of the problem is the lack of BIPAL representation in the ideas, the culture, and the daily operations of the company. The lack of diversity gives way to repressive silence. The ethos of the company is based in whiteness.

The use of a group email leverages shame to garner support for the author's position. Calling the Black woman "angry" for pointing out racism that exists within the company is capitalizing on a racial stereotype. Attempting to make white people the victim in this scenario is gaslighting.

Interrupting the Racism: **"Reply all" to the email and identify the racism in the original email. Close the email by restating the issue that was raised at the meeting and the facts to support it. Do not apologize for the behavior of the sender of the email. Hold the white person accountable without making excuses or implying intent. Demand the sender of the email "reply all" with a full and unconditional apology to the Black woman.**

Scenario 2: *A corporate group that includes people across lines of racial difference is taking an intercultural competency workshop. They engage in the following exercise: Each participant is asked to name their favorite food their family makes at holidays or special celebrations; then they are asked to share with the group who in their family is known for making it, how it came to be a part of their family's traditions, and how it represents their culture. After everyone shares, the facilitator says, "Each one of us has different traditions that are important to us based in our culture, but all of us share the experience of how food brings us all together. By focusing not on what makes us different but what makes us alike, we can build the bridges necessary to heal the deepest divisions among us."*

In 2017 Pepsi aired a commercial featuring Kendall Jenner. The commercial's backdrop was of a protest of injustice. Kendall's character leaves her modeling photo shoot to join the protest. While walking alongside other protesters, she fist bumps a participant, then walks out of the crowd to a line of police officers, opens a can of Pepsi, and offers it to one of the officers. After drinking from the open can, the police officer then turns to his colleague and smiles. Kendall returns to the protestors, and everyone cheers as if this can of Pepsi fixes the racialized terror that made the protest necessary. Pepsi mistakenly centers itself as the "shared experience that brings us all together," just like the food in the intercultural competency workshop. Neither Pepsi nor the food erase the history and harm of racism. Workshops, even those that are deemed interculturally competent and that claim this is true, perpetuate racism instead.

Interrupting the Racism: This training is palatable and digestible to those who wish to deny that racism is a dividing factor. What this scenario suggests is that if we do not focus on racism, it will miraculously go away. It does not get to the root of the issue, it erases the differences of each participant, and it relegates the brilliance of human difference to happenstance. Refuse, at all costs, the temptation to take comfort only in our similarities. Rather, name the specifics of difference as assets and the ways they are used as a tool of racism to harm.

Scenario 3: *A Latina/x woman pastor appointed to a white-dominant church speaks out about her experiences of racism there. The supervising pastor, a BIPAL person, diminishes her testimony of harm by stating, "These are her experiences. This is what* she thinks, *but this is not an indictment against you as a church. Do you understand what I am saying?"*

What we see here is what is rarely discussed in anti-racism trainings: internalized racism. Usually, in anti-racism trainings this is not discussed because the racial identities of the participants vary. However, it exists! As BIPAL people, we are conditioned, and as there are with most things there are nuances to this. The above scenario displays internalized racism—a consequence of racism.

The BIPAL supervising pastor goes on to coddle the white congregation by dismissing the experiences of the Latina/x woman. His statement casts doubt on her in an effort to make the white congregants comfortable. His concern focuses on the viability of the church and relieving their white manipulation (fragility), at the expense of the Latina/x pastor's well-being. His comments protected the white church, leaving the Latina/x woman open to more attacks because they knew at that point that she was not protected or cared for.

<u>Interrupting the Racism</u>: **Members of the congregation who are aware of the racialized terror experienced by the pastor should speak out in defense of the pastor: "I know this happened because I witnessed it." "I believe her." White congregations should take measures to ensure that they publicly denounce oppressive behaviors and create action steps to be taken if such occurrences of racism happen to anyone within their community.**

For the pastor who is harmed, the following script could be used to address the supervising pastor:

By my own testimony—verbal and in writing in multiple settings now—I have provided ample evidence of individual, interpersonal, and institutional racism that have occurred since my appointment here. [Name specific instances here.] Your insistence that the specific harm done to me is limited to "my experiences" and "not an indictment" of the church or its people highlighted for me your priority to protect the viability of the church over and against your duties as a supervising pastor to serve as pastor to the pastors in your assigned area. I am looking for specific, concrete support from you to address the racism of the congregation and the harm done to me.

ACTION-NOW Learning Engagement
REAL TIME: Brainstorming Scenarios and Scripts

Below, a number of expressions of racism are named. After each example, use the box attached to [1] name the racism perpetrated and [2] write out a script you could use to interrupt that form of racism the next time you encounter it. As you write your own scripts, keep these things in mind:

- **Racism must be interrupted in the moment**: Note when in the scenario you would speak or act, how late is too late, when an interruption takes the form of silence, and how your racial identity dictates what your interruption is in each scenario. What, if any, personal hesitations that currently hold us back from interrupting racism in REAL TIME must be overcome—and how will you overcome them?
- **Anti-racism must be enacted immediately after learning what to do/not to do**: What learning or experiences of anti-racism inform the content as well as the method you use to interrupt racism? If you do not interrupt racism in the moment, make sure to prepare for the next time by researching, planning, and role-playing the anti-racism.
- **Anti-racists must see preparation and practice as necessary to get ready, be ready, and stay ready:** We *do not* role-play the racism, especially in groups across racial difference. Role-played racism creates the harm of racism. For people who are unfamiliar with a particular form of racism or who have trouble recognizing it in the moment, Google it; unfortunately, there are plenty of examples we can find with a simple search.
- **For those of us who are white:** We must always consider it our responsibility to interrupt racism in REAL TIME unless directed not to do so by a BIPAL person or strategy.
- **For BIPAL people:** Our responsibility is not to shield, protect, or try to explain away the racism or harm in each scenario.

WRITE YOUR RESPONSE BELOW: *Name two ways you will overcome a personal hesitation to interrupting racism in real time in the upcoming week:*

Scenario 1: *An Asian woman attends a community meeting gathered to discuss ways to "be a better neighbor" to one another. The discussion moves to COVID, precautions, and the ways that racism has created different health, economic, and social consequences of COVID based in racial identity. Hearing this, she specifically highlights the term "Chinese virus" as harmful and racist. She shares experiences of her own and those of her children and how isolated they feel from their community that once embraced them. She also mentions how she doesn't always know how she "fits" within conversations about racism that only talk about "Black and white."*

Scenario 2: *At an anti-racism rally, a number of leaders of social justice and church organizations were invited to speak. A white male president of a national social justice religious organization was one of the speakers. He had a wide range of accomplishments on his resume and in his work as president, leading a diverse group of Christian denominations to work together. However, he had no proven or documented evidence of anti-racism work to his credit— either vocational or personal. His speech invited all gathered to rely on love to unify us, cautioned against focusing on our differences, and highlighted exemplary People of Color who have done the work of bringing people together in the face of hatred, including the Reverend Dr. Martin Luther King Jr.*

Scenario 3: *A well-known organization tapped four (4) of their employees to represent their company at an annual meeting. The flier was distributed via social media and other venues. The description next to each employee's name and picture, except for the Pacific-Islander woman, included their official title and function within the company (for example, Director of Personnel, FIRST NAME LAST NAME). The Pacific-Islander woman's information listed her name and title based on her marital status (Mrs. FIRST NAME LAST NAME) even though she was selected specifically for her skill set based on her role in the company.*

Scenario 4: *A keynote speaker (or guest preacher) says something racist during their presentation (or sermon).*

** 4REALS-written scripts and responses to the aforementioned scenarios can be found in Appendix A on page ##.

Chapter 5:

REAL CHANGE: B.E. Change

> REAL CHANGE crafts accountability templates and measures to ensure that tangible, meaningful, and powerful change for racial justice replaces good intentions and workshops. REAL CHANGE requires that we focus on outcome, not on intent. REAL CHANGE provides ways to track, assess, and analyze successes and failures (yes, failures), and make on-the-go shifts that avoid the most common roadblocks and obstacles to anti-racism work. REAL CHANGE creates methods of accountability and transparency that build not only timelines and momentum but also trust. REAL CHANGE provides the external measurements and an accountability paradigm that brings all people the opportunity to participate in anti-racism that is actually anti-racist.

Because REAL CHANGE requires action, this chapter is set up a little bit differently. Our racially positioned responses are shorter so that we can offer more space for templates of accountability, assessment, and action. We've had REAL TALK and offered REAL STRATEGIES for anti-racism work in REAL TIME. Now is the time to assess what has been done and stand accountable for what has not. Now is the time to put the words, intentions, and practice into measurable steps. Now is the time to assess whether our talk has become our walk. REAL CHANGE is where anti-racism becomes anti-racist. This chapter is set up to provide multiple ways for that to occur.

REV. BECKFORD'S RESPONSE: The movie *One Night in Miami* inspired the subtitle for this chapter: B.E. Change. As the film title suggests, the movie takes place on one night in Miami, where four famous Black men meet in a hotel room to enjoy a historic victory. Sam Cooke (a musician),

Muhammad Ali (a boxer, also known as Cassius Clay), Jim Brown (an NFL star turned actor), and the Honorable Malcom X (a Nation of Islam civil rights activist) gather to celebrate Cassius Clay's boxing win, but that's not all. The festive evening begins with change. The hotel room where they stay is not filled with people, alcohol, loud music, or dancing, as we would expect at a celebration of an event of this magnitude. Instead, the four men share their desires, hopes, fears, and beliefs. The Honorable Malcolm X uses this entry point to speak with his friends about using the power their platforms afford them. By the final scene of the movie, each person has done just that.

The subtitle of this chapter is "B.E. Change." Here, the *B.E.* stands for "Beyond Excuses." In anti-racism work, every single one of us must push beyond excuses. BIPAL people are always accused of making excuses for not pulling ourselves up by our bootstraps. We are often told that we use excuses such as "we're paid less" or "the hiring practices are discriminatory" to defend why we don't advance in the workplace or in life. But 4REALS is talking about something different here. Excuses are reasons for avoiding responsibility without factual foundation. These are not excuses—these are facts based in racist policies, procedures, and practices. Structural oppression plays a major role in how our communities bang against glass ceilings. What are often categorized as excuses that BIPAL people use to avoid succeeding or thriving are actually the realities of institutional and systemic racism that we must push against in order to dislodge, disrupt, and dismantle it.

For BIPAL people, the excuses that prevent REAL CHANGE are the following:

- No one will listen to me, so there's no use in trying
- I am a BIPAL person, so I don't need anti-racism work; by nature, I am anti-racist
- We don't have the resources to combat whiteness

The fact remains: If or when we do the bidding of whiteness so it can prevail, we are not anti-racist. At the same time, we are not racist because we do not have the power to uphold or change policies. However—and this is often overlooked—we can participate in racist behaviors that advance the agendas and systems that perpetrate racialized terror.

To do the kind of REAL CHANGE that goes beyond excuses, it is important that we admit to ourselves our participation in excuse-making.

FOR BIPAL PEOPLE ONLY, WRITE YOUR RESPONSE BELOW: *Note any excuses you have used in the past that have prevented you from using your opportunities or platforms to make a difference.*

White people also make excuses for themselves as to why they are not engaged in anti-racism work. These reasons, however, are not grounded in systemic racism functioning to oppress white people. Thus, these are actual excuses; they are literally used to excuse white people from doing what is necessary because of discomfort, risk, manipulation, or fear. Some examples follow:

- We are not wanted in anti-racism work; we get rejected by BIPAL people when we try
- That is not our work to do
- We need more information/education
- I do not know what to say or do; I say nothing to be on the safe side
- This is how I was raised

FOR WHITE PEOPLE ONLY, WRITE YOUR RESPONSE BELOW: *Note all reasons you have used to excuse you from engaging in anti-racism work.*

When we are honest with ourselves, we find that most of what holds us back from REAL CHANGE are excuses. For BIPAL people, some are actually realities based in structural racism meant to oppress us but misnamed as excuses, while others are actual excuses. For white people excuses serve as defense mechanisms meant to distance them from their responsibility and the benefits they reap. For each of us, REAL CHANGE requires admitting our excuses as a first step. For all of us, REAL CHANGE requires us to push BEYOND EXCUSES.

REV. LEDDER'S RESPONSE: It's one thing to talk about wanting change; it's another to do what is necessary to enact it. REAL CHANGE requires more than intent, more than slogans, more than the latest lingo, more than research, more than workshops, and more than another book study. REAL CHANGE requires a transformation, such that what has been remains no longer.

In terms of anti-racism, REAL CHANGE is the consequence of actually interrupting and dismantling racism. REAL CHANGE can recognize, name, locate, describe, and explain with proven evidence that racism has been interrupted and/or dismantled. For this, measures of accountability, assessment, and action are necessary. For those of us who are white, this is where the proverbial rubber hits the road. If change does not occur in tangible, meaningful, and powerful ways according to BIPAL people, we are not doing anti-racism work. Thus, our claims to believe in anti-racism, to desire racism's demise, and to risk whatever it takes to stand for what is just, stand or fall based on whether REAL CHANGE has occurred.

REAL CHANGE demands proof of intentions, proof of actions, and proof of anti-racism. REAL CHANGE takes many forms but is extinct without evidence. White people must be capable of doing whatever needs to be done to interrupt and dismantle racism by any means necessary. We will do so by obeying the REAL STRATEGIES created or cosigned by BIPAL people, and we will implement them in REAL TIME. REAL CHANGE places all of our promises to want to do good, to do good, and to be about the good in full view and asks, "But did we do it?" REAL CHANGE refuses to allow those of us who are white to rest in any form of pretense that does not actuate anti-racism. REAL CHANGE is an accounting of our actions or inactions and will not accept plans, goals, or action steps as bond. REAL CHANGE reminds white people that we do not have the luxury of being white and not engaging anti-racism work on a deliberate, deliverable level. REAL CHANGE exposes all of our excuses and claims that we "meant to" and calls us into accountability, responsibility, and consequence. REAL CHANGE asks us what we've been doing with all of our information gathering and listening, what risks and responsibilities we've taken, and how we've obeyed the strategies of BIPAL people. REAL

TALK is just more talk without REAL CHANGE. REAL STRATEGIES are just to-do lists without REAL CHANGE. REAL TIME is just another distraction without REAL CHANGE. Anti-racism is racism in a pretty mask without REAL CHANGE.

On a scale from 1 to 10, with 1 being the least amount of work and 10 being the greatest, how much anti-racism REAL CHANGE do you believe you have enacted since you began reading this book?

1   2   3   4   5   6   7   8   9   10

Explain to someone who hasn't read the book why you answered the way you did on the previous question.

Out of all the anti-racism options and strategies this book has listed thus far, what percentage do you think you've enacted since you started reading this book?

How, if at all, does this align with your first answer (1–10) above?

ACTION-NOW Learning Engagement:
REAL TEMPLATES FOR CHANGE

REAL CHANGE requires a sustainable revolution in policies, procedures, power, and practice. Making policy changes without enforcing them keeps the practices of oppression intact. This level of sustainability requires transparent accountability and undisputable commitment. For accountability, assessment, and action to occur, we need some sort of method for measurement. Anti-Racism 4REALS believes in templates that not only determine whether or not racism has been interrupted or dismantled but also serve as a roadmap for enacting the necessary work. The following set of REAL CHANGE templates creates a number of entry points for interrupting and dismantling racism and for creating accountability, transparency, and trust. The templates provided here follow the same principles as all the other ACTION-NOW Learning Engagements: You can start to use them as soon as you finish the chapter, leave the workshop, or click "leave meeting." Each can be adapted for nonprofits, business corporations, schools, government agencies, neighborhoods, and more. For more customized work, Anti-Racism 4REALS offers a number of workshops and consulting packages to help any group utilize these and other custom-built templates to actualize anti-racism work in context.

While this is not an exhaustive list, the pages that follow provide a diverse range of opportunities to engage in anti-racism with REAL TALK and REAL STRATEGIES in REAL TIME. Each REAL CHANGE template includes instructions, nuances for contextualization, and a worksheet model for notes, plans, and accountability. Let's get started!

REAL LIST 4 REAL CHANGE

INSTRUCTIONS: In Appendix B you will find a list of anti-racism strategies, ideas, and ACTION-NOW Learning Engagements listed in Anti-Racism 4REALS. For a refresher, you can go to the page number(s) listed before beginning the strategy. A box for notes below serves as a template you can use to list any of the following: [1] how you have utilized this strategy thus far; [2] what internal or external resistance you have experienced regarding this strategy; [3] what your plan is to enact this strategy; [4] to whom will you be accountable for enacting this strategy; or [5] what this strategy's contextualized interruption and dismantling of racism in your church, community, school, business, or otherwise will be. Utilize this ACTION-NOW Learning Engagement to track your anti-racism work and to create a longer-term anti-racist anti-racism strategy.

Name of Strategy:

Pages:

How have you utilized this strategy thus far?

What internal or external resistance have you experienced regarding this strategy?

What is your plan for enacting this strategy?

Who will be accountable to whom for enacting this strategy? How does this follow the overall template for doing anti-racism work (BIPAL people create or cosign strategy, white people enact all of it except specific actions designated for only BIPAL people, and white people are accountable to BIPAL people to determine faithfulness and effectiveness of work)?

Name of Strategy:

Pages:

How have you utilized this strategy thus far?

What internal or external resistance have you experienced regarding this strategy?

What is your plan for enacting this strategy?

Who will be accountable to whom for enacting this strategy? How does this follow the overall template for doing anti-racism work (BIPAL people create or cosign strategy, white people enact all of it except specific actions designated for only BIPAL people, and white people are accountable to BIPAL people to determine faithfulness and effectiveness of work)?

Name of Strategy:

Pages:

How have you utilized this strategy thus far?

What internal or external resistance have you experienced regarding this strategy?

What is your plan for enacting this strategy?

Who will be accountable to whom for enacting this strategy? How does this follow the overall template for doing anti-racism work (BIPAL people create or cosign strategy, white people enact all of it except specific actions designated for only BIPAL people, and white people are accountable to BIPAL people to determine faithfulness and effectiveness of work)?

Name of Strategy:

Pages:

How have you utilized this strategy thus far?

What internal or external resistance have you experienced regarding this strategy?

What is your plan for enacting this strategy?

Who will be accountable to whom for enacting this strategy? How does this follow the overall template for doing anti-racism work (BIPAL people create or cosign strategy, white people enact all of it except specific actions designated for only BIPAL people, and white people are accountable to BIPAL people to determine faithfulness and effectiveness of work)?

DEVELOPING AN EQUITY MODEL

Equity works to repair the historic, ongoing, and compounding harm of racism and racialized discrimination. Equity models serve as guideposts, accountability templates, and interpretive lenses by which organizations of any sort can create racial equity in policy, procedure, practice, and power. The following ten questions can get you started. Your answers provide the entry points both for goals and for the work needed to get you there.

1. What is the difference between equality and equity?
2. How does this model decenter whiteness?
3. How does this model ensure that racially equitable policies are adhered to regardless of an individual's personal stance?
4. Create a list of the names and titles of the most powerful decision makers in your organization. Next to each name write the person's racial identity. How does this represent ongoing racism or an anti-racism culture?
5. How many policies have been written from the lens of anti-racism? How do you know?
6. How do you measure pay equity? How are issues of pay inequity remedied?
7. What is necessary to remove all implicit and explicit racialized bias from the position, promotion, and leadership requirements of your organization?
8. What process is necessary to identify and remove all racialized bias from your organizational training and onboarding?
9. What policies and accountability are in place to ensure leaders of your organization have proven evidence of anti-racism training, skills, and outcomes?
10. What five things can you do right now to create a foundation of an anti-racism culture in your organization that reflects equity?

CREATING A MORE RACIALLY DIVERSE
BOARD OR LEADERSHIP GROUP

When white-dominant organizations recognize their need for a more racially diverse board or leadership group, models of "diversity" and "inclusion" fall short by doing harm in many ways—including perpetrating more racism. The mini ACTION-NOW Learning Engagement below will help you identify the current thinking strategies of your organization and provide a five-step anti-racist anti-racism template to honorably create a more racially diverse board or leadership group.

Mini ACTION-NOW Learning Engagement:

You can do this exercise alone, with a group, or with a set of small groups.

Imagine you are creating a racially diverse twelve-member board or leadership group for your church, social justice group, organization, school, or business. Think very specifically about race, the racial identities of the members, the racial demographics of the surrounding community, the history of your group and its leadership, and the qualifications for leadership you want the members to have. Take between five and fifteen minutes to brainstorm and list the racialized makeup of the new board or leadership group. Be prepared to discuss with others how you came up with the list and how you would make the changes between the current all-white or white-dominant group and the new one. Include also, if you can, how decisions were anti-racist.

After brainstorming and creating your list, answer the following prompts.

List the racial makeup of the group:

How did you decide the new racial makeup of the group?

What about the new racial makeup makes this more diverse board/leadership group anti-racist?

What about your process and/or the new racial makeup makes the process honorable?

CREATING A MORE RACIALLY DIVERSE
BOARD OR LEADERSHIP GROUP: DEBRIEF

Rev. Ledder has done this learning engagement during her tenure at GCORR. In all the times she has led it, not one time did a group create and describe a board or leadership group that was 100 percent BIPAL people. Not once. This includes groups who have a well-documented and known history of boards/leadership groups that have been 100 percent white for years. Consider again the equality model versus the equity model. Equity addresses past and current inequality but doesn't use equality models to address it. Racialized equitable boards and leadership groups will use methods that don't seem "fair" according to the equality model (in which every share/risk/opportunity is of equal measure). Rather, equity requires justice, and justice requires new percentages and strategies that cannot make up for past and current inequality but that begin to make some recompense for injustice and harm.

Five Action Items to Honorably Create a More Racially Diverse Board or Leadership Group:

1. Require all current board/leadership group members to submit their resignations and reapply for selection. Rewrite selection criteria to require proven evidence of anti-racism work. Anti-racism work will include BIPAL people's lived experiences resisting racism directed at them and their communities.
2. Determine the number of years the board/leadership group has been in existence. Determine an average number of members of each board/group. Multiply these together. Determine to the best of your ability the number of BIPAL people who have served thus far in your organization's history. Subtract the number of BIPAL people from the total to calculate how many terms white people have served. How many terms would the board have to consist of 100 percent BIPAL people before the number of white people's terms and BIPAL people's terms were equal?
3. What excuses would you have to refute or counter if the new policy were to mandate 100 percent BIPAL people on the board / in the leadership group for the next five years?
4. Create time, agenda structure, and the priorities of the board/ leadership group meetings based on guidance from BIPAL people in your organization.

5. Pay all BIPAL people for their board/leadership group service. Refute or counter claims that no one gets paid for their service with the following argument:
    a. No one gets paid for the work of the board (whatever that is).
    b. BIPAL people are being paid for additional work they do on top of what everyone is doing as their board/leadership group service. This work includes the following:
        i. racially diversifying the group (BIPAL people are required for this to occur—this is something white people cannot do on their own)
        ii. withstanding the harm of micro- and macro-aggressions while the white members learn anti-racism
        iii. teaching the white members about anti-racism, including but not limited to the racism the white members enact (also enduring white members' white manipulation—otherwise known as white fragility)
        iv. creating or cosigning anti-racist anti-racism strategies for the board/leadership group to engage as practice or policy or organization

Five Action Steps to Honorably Create a More Racially Diverse Board of Leadership Group

		Example
1. Number of years the board or leadership group has been in existence	_____	100
2. Average number of members on the Board at a time	_____	10
3. Multiply to get the number of "spots" available until now	_____	100 x 10 = 1000
4. Number of BIPAL people who have served thus far in the organization's history	_____	5
5. Subtract the number of terms BIPAL people have served	_____	(4) 2 for years (3) 3 for 1 year 7 terms

Total "Spots" (1000) minus BIPAL terms (7) = 993

Thus, 99 years of 100% BIPAL terms to "catch up".

CREATE AN ANTI-RACIST BUDGET

It has been said that if we want to know what is important to a person or organization, we should look at their budget. This is because we spend and allocate our money to that which we deem worthy. Budgets can perpetrate racism explicitly and implicitly—from money spent to fund racially unjust endeavors, to charitable donations, to vendor decisions. Use the checklist below to create a budget using anti-racist strategies with an anti-racist lens. Start with an existing budget or create one anew.

Prompt Questions:

1. How does your organization vet vendors?
   - What does it mean to be an anti-racist organization?
   - How would you know whether an organization is anti-racist?
   - A company based in a racially diverse city has fifteen employees, only two of whom are BIPAL people who hold managerial positions. There are no other BIPAL employees. Does this fit an anti-racist model? No, a seven-to-one ratio doesn't make it anti-racist.
   - A company based in a white community with two BIPAL families has fifteen employees, one of whom is a BIPAL person. Does this fit an anti-racist model? It could! Even though in this example there is only one person instead of two, based on the racial demographics of the community the representation of BIPAL people is statistically higher. Additional questions should include whether the BIPAL person is expected to conform to the standards of whiteness (for example, repressive silence).

2. Have BIPAL people contributed to the creation of your budget?
   - If not, why? What excuses have been used to justify this?
   - Name the racial identities of the people on your budget committees.
   - How do you know the strategies and priorities of BIPAL people are honored in your budget?

3. Is there funding for anti-racism work?
   - How do you define anti-racism work? What qualifies?
   - Specifically, what percentage of your budget contributes directly to creating and protecting an anti-racism culture in your company?
   - Who makes the final decisions regarding funding? What if any changes need to be made?

4. Is there racial equity in salaries?
   - Review the current salaries and disaggregate (separate by component parts) by race.
   - Determine the difference between equality and equity. Use the model that addresses past and current inequalities in

salary based on race.
- Readjust budget accordingly.

5. <u>Transfer or switch all financial accounts to economic institutions run by and/or owned by BIPAL people.</u>

- Transfer your credit cards, bank accounts, mortgages, and investments.
- White people: Avoid opening or transferring accounts to BIPAL-owned credit unions, especially Black-owned credit unions. Credit unions are owned by the account holders. Flooding the credit union with accounts owned by white people changes the ownership status.

CONCLUSION

There is no half-hearted solution that will dislodge, disrupt, and dismantle racism. Yes, 4REALS has spent the entirety of these pages introducing entry points to challenge everyone into action right now. We do this to refute the lie that some people aren't ready, or that anti-racism prerequisites must be satisfied before doing something, or that the work is so great that silence or unresponsiveness is acceptable. If anything, for us, this speaks to the reality that racism, and the work to dismantle it, is enormous, entrenched, and escalating. Racism is brutality levied against BIPAL people *so that* those of us who are white may survive, thrive, and succeed at their expense.

WRITE YOUR RESPONSE BELOW, FOR EVERYONE: *What was your initial response to the last sentence? Especially consider your logical, emotional, and physical reaction to the words "so that."*

WRITE YOUR RESPONSE BELOW, FOR WHITE PEOPLE: *Record internal or explicit counterarguments that come up for you here. After doing so, write down which aspect of racism is connected to each counterargument. What do you need to do to interrupt and dismantle your attachment to this aspect of racism?*

Counter Argument	Aspect of Racism	Dismantle Attachment

Although entry points and REAL STRATEGIES provide multiple opportunities for anyone to do the work of anti-racism right now, it's equally important to stay focused on the system of racism and how it functions. To do so, we must hold two major categories in tandem. Racism has many expressions, and examples can be discussed using two overarching categories. Individual or interpersonal racism focuses on beliefs, values, and actions held within a person or expressed within a relationship (either professional or personal). Institutional or systemic racism focuses on policies, practices, and procedures that perpetrate racism within an institution (such as a church, the American banking system, or higher education) or across institutions (for example, racialized discrimination in banking affects who receives mortgages, which affects who builds home equity, which affects local school funding and higher education choices).

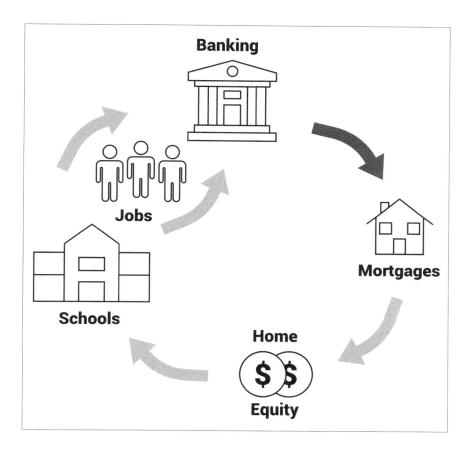

Both categories must be addressed. The constant call for the heart to be changed before the policies will change sounds *real* good. However, addressing institutional/systemic racism without addressing individual/interpersonal racism can lead to hypocrisy—policies on paper that don't interrupt racist decisions, or promotions based in the racialized discrimination coded in language like "managerial discretion" or "culture fit." Changing policies without changing those in power only drives people to find creative ways to circumvent such policies. The logic of racism surmises that we must focus on individual and interpersonal racism for institutional/systemic anti-racism to stick. Furthermore, especially in white-dominant groups, the focus shifts solely to the individual/interpersonal *until* people have been prepared to create and protect the changes necessary for institutional/systemic equity and justice. But here's the thing:

107

> *There is no automatic pathway between*
> *individual/interpersonal anti-racism &*
> *institutional/systemic anti-racism*

REAL TALK: Did you think that this was going to be just another book study? You have read through each chapter of Anti-Racism 4REALS: REAL TALK with REAL STRATEGIES in REAL TIME for REAL CHANGE. However, anti-racist anti-racism work requires that each of us applies the ACTION-NOW Learning Engagements and other strategies found within these pages to our REAL lives.

WRITE YOUR RESPONSE BELOW: *Have you ever been told to write the significant facts or points of a book in the margins so you can go back to them? We ask that you go back to those initial feelings, beliefs, and questions you had as you read through this book. Next, identify the areas or times in your life where you participated in racial discrimination or perpetrated racism.*

Absorbing information *about* anti-racism without *application of* anti-racism is useless. To engage with this book as just another book study without applying the information learned is a waste of time and wisdom. Take a moment to use the strategy of practice to commit to making Anti-Racism 4REALS a daily practice and lifelong work. Two options to begin with can be found below.

The first is a commitment letter written by you to yourself. Add specifics based on your racial positionality and how it influences how you will honorably do the work of anti-racism.

Dear,

I have read the book Anti-Racism 4REALS and committed to practice the strategies I've learned while engaging in anti-racism work. I recognize that I have practiced, perpetrated, or participated in actions or inactions rooted in white supremacy. These actions furthered the harm caused to BIPAL people (or to my community, for BIPAL people). I will continue to use these anti-racism strategies generally:

1. _____ ,
2. _____ ,
3. _____ .

In order to specifically dislodge, disrupt, and dismantle racism *in my personal life*, I commit to the following anti-racist strategies:

1. _____ ,
2. _____ ,
3. _____ .

I also commit to these strategies specifically to dislodge, disrupt, and dismantle racism *within systems*:

1. _____ ,
2. _____ ,
3. _____
_____ , _____ or _____ .

When I falter, because I will, I will hold myself accountable by moving beyond excuses to correct my actions and apologize to those I have harmed. I understand that these next steps will require resistance, resiliency, courage, and—in some cases—consequences, yet I commit myself to doing this critical and necessary work.

Signed, _____ DATE _____

The second opportunity for anti-racist commitments includes actions with your community.

Create a list of anti-racism actions that your primary community has engaged in the last six months. Of those, label which fall into the category of individual/interpersonal and which fall into the category of institutional/systemic. Analyze the list for imbalances. Does the individual/interpersonal anti-racism work eclipse or distract from policy changes and institutional accountability?

Does the focus on institutional/systemic racism still allow space or create permission for individual/interpersonal racism to exist? If so, in what ways?

What changes need to be made in order to ensure that your community is creating an anti-racist culture instead of attempting to complete an anti-racist checklist or to-do list?

You have come to the final chapter of *Anti-Racism 4REALS: Real Talk with Real Strategies in Real Time for Real Change*, but the work of anti-racism continues. It continues beyond the appendices, and after you close the book or shut off your device. The work of anti-racism must continue until racism has been dislodged, disrupted, and dismantled. In order for anti-racism to happen in REAL life, each of us must continue to engage in REAL TALK with REAL STRATEGIES in REAL TIME for REAL CHANGE.

> *"We who believe in freedom cannot rest until it comes."*
> *—Sweet Honey in the Rock*

> *"Freedom cannot be until racism is* no more.*"*
> *—4REALS, LLC.*

Appendix A

REAL TIME SCENARIOS: AUTHORS' RESPONSES

Scenario 1: *An Asian woman attends a community meeting gathered to discuss ways to "be a better neighbor" to one another. The discussion moves to COVID, precautions, and the ways that racism has created different health, economic, and social consequences of COVID based in racial identity. Hearing this, she specifically highlights the term "Chinese virus" as harmful and racist. She shares experiences of her own and those of her children and how isolated they feel from their community that once embraced them. She also mentions how she doesn't always know how she "fits" within conversations about racism that only talk about "Black and white."*

Example Response:

Racism in any of its forms is always wrong/evil/unjust [use any term depending on language authentic to your identity]. That you and your family have been the direct and indirect targets of racism is unacceptable. As a community we must be willing and capable of shutting down all racial slurs, including but not limited to the one you just mentioned, which falsely blames China and Chinese people for COVID. Anti-Black racism, Anti-Asian or Anti-Pacific-Islander racism, and all other forms of racism are based in white supremacy, which pits BIPAL people against each other in order to avoid addressing the real injustices and oppression of racism. As a community, we can be neighbors only when we refuse to allow any racism or racialized prejudice to harm any BIPAL person.

Scenario 2: *At an anti-racism rally, a number of leaders of social justice and church organizations were invited to speak. A white male president of a national social justice religious organization was one of the speakers. He had a wide range of accomplishments on his resume and in his work as president, leading a diverse group of Christian denominations to work together. However,* *he had no proven or documented evidence of anti-racism work to his credit— either vocational or personal. His speech invited all gathered to rely on love to unify us, cautioned against focusing on our differences, and highlighted exemplary People of Color who have done the work of bringing people together in the face of hatred, including the Reverend Dr. Martin Luther King Jr.*

Example Responses:

1. Organize a chant to disrupt speech in REAL TIME:
   a. "Racism isn't interrupted by love alone!"
   b. "Some of the worst racism is perpetrated by white moderates!" (This is based on the Reverend Dr. Martin Luther King Jr.'s Letter from Birmingham Jail.)
   c. "Unity doesn't equal equity!"
   d. "Racial justice requires anti-racism!"
   e. "Justice is what love looks like in public!" (This is from Dr. Cornel West.)

2. Use social media to amplify the event's hashtag and add critiques of the "unity and love" message, which cannot interrupt and dismantle racism.

3. Write opinion pieces for papers, blogs, Medium, academia, and social media feeds that critique the model of "love and unity," which attempts to ignore or erase the realities of racism. Include five specific anti-racism strategies found in Appendix B instead. (Here is one way you can cite this book as a source: Beckford, Sheila M., and E. Michelle Ledder. Anti-Racism 4REALS: Real Talk with Real Strategies in Real Time for Real Change. Nashville: Chalice Press, 2021.)

4. Contact the organizers of the event. Challenge them to rewrite their procedures and practices for speaker invitations to include requirements for proven evidence of anti-racism work and outcomes (not just social justice work in general) that must be fulfilled in order for a person to be invited to speak about anti-racism or to address racism.

5. Contact the speaker. Tell him your concerns about "love and unity" as a method that does not lead to interrupting and dismantling racism. Send him a copy of this book, or direct him to the 4REALS website for training or consulting for anti-racism work, future speeches, or workshops for his organizations.

Scenario 3: *A well-known organization tapped four (4) of their employees to represent their company at an annual meeting. The flier was distributed via social media and other venues. The description next to each employee's name and picture, except for the Pacific-Islander woman, included their official title and function within the company (for example, Director of Personnel, FIRST NAME LAST NAME). The Pacific-Islander woman's information listed her name and title based on her marital status (Mrs. FIRST NAME LAST NAME) even though she was selected specifically for her skill set based on her role in the company.*

Example Response:

Dear [NAME],

There are four people listed on this flier. All have been listed with their positions within the company except for [TITLE FIRST NAME LAST NAME], who is a Pacific Islander person. She is listed on this flier with the title *Mrs.*, as if you tapped her to speak about marriage and not to share the expertise she has to offer in her role as [POSITION]. She has been chosen to present because of her proficiency in her role in the company.

Please remove this post and retract the flier from other social media platforms, redo the flier, and repost it. Please also offer [TITLE FIRST NAME LAST NAME] an apology for the racist and sexist nature of the flier.

Scenario 4: *A keynote speaker (or guest preacher) says something racist during their presentation (or sermon).*

Example Response 1:

Walk out.

Response 2:

During the sermon, interrupt the preacher:

- "Hold up, preacher. You're going too far to the right."
- "That's not the gospel of Jesus, it's the gospel of Jim Crow."
- "Bring it back now."

Response 3:

Interrupt the speaker or preacher: "Nope, that's racist."

Response 4:

"Wait! That statement was a racist comment. You owe all of us sitting here an apology."

<u>Response 5</u>:

"As the organizer for this event, I must interject and inform you that your last statement was racist and derogatory. Please apologize to the guests who are here. We will resume our program. The next person who will grace the mic is [NAME]."

Appendix B

LIST OF STRATEGIES

The following is a list of 137 strategies, anti-racist ideas, and AC-TION-NOW Learning Engagements that can be used right away. Use the prompt below, the page number(s) associated with it, and the interpretive question "How can I use this to interrupt and dismantle racism?" to enact anti-racism by engaging in REAL TALK with REAL STRATEGIES in REAL TIME for REAL CHANGE.

1. Interrogate your assumptions about leaders' (religious, social justice, nonprofit, or otherwise) willingness, commitment to, and abilities for anti-racism. (Intro, blue box, p. 2)

2. How have you refuted the lie that colorblindness ("I don't see color") is anti-racist? (Introduction, p. 4)

3. How have your actions reflected the reality that more talk promotes harm, while REAL TALK interrupts harm? (Introduction, p. 6)

4. For white people: Use the phrase "for those of us who are white" to avoid trying to separate us from our whiteness and from "those other white people," or trying to pretend that we are somehow outside of the system of racism even while we do anti-racism work. (Introduction, pp. 6-7)

5. White people: Reduce our talking time and our need for others to pay attention to our experiences, feelings, and strategies. (introduction, p. 7)

6. Avoid "workshop hoarding" that collects information about anti-racism instead of doing the work of anti-racism. (Introduction, p. 7 & REAL STRATEGIES pp. 41-42)

7. Correct the misinterpretation of Matthew 18:15–17a and teach how faithful interpretations do the work of anti-racism (pp. 8-9)

8. Only role-play the interruption of the racism, not the racism itself. (Introduction, p. 9, REAL TIME p. 66 for fuller description)

9. Create and utilize anti-racist covenants in general and interrogation questions. (ANLE, pp. 16-17)

10. Assume humanity and build trust. (Introduction, Anti-Racist Covenant, p. 18)

11. Do anti-racism work based in racial positionality and take on associated challenges. (Anti-Racist Covenant, p. 18 & REAL STRATEGIES pp. 47-48)

12. Recognize and avoid using "good-sounding words" that actually do harm. (Anti-Racist Covenant, p. 18)

13. Evaluate your (or your organization's) no-tolerance policy regarding violence. Determine how racism is or is not considered violence in terms of the policy or stance. (REAL TALK, pp. 20-21)

14. In terms of racism and anti-racism, what is "the talk?" In what ways can it replicate racism, and in what ways can it repudiate racism? (REAL TALK, pp. 22-23)

15. For white people: Eliminate all uses of white protective silence. For BIPAL people: Eliminate the need to respond to demands for speech or to make excuses for white protective silence. (REAL TALK, pp. 25-26)

16. Ensure you use and understand the phrase "silence is violence" in ways that do anti-racism work and do not perpetrate racism. (REAL TALK, pp. 26-28)

17. For white people: Interrupt racism in the midst of the meeting. (REAL TALK, p. 29)

18. Refuse to offer "thoughts and prayers" without any substantial and concrete measures of anti-racist action accompanying them. (REAL TALK, p. 30)

19. Refuse to use prayer as a way to protect white people from the discomfort of addressing racism. (REAL TALK, pp. 30-31)

20. Engage in anti-racist holy silence. (REAL TALK, ACTION-NOW Learning Engagement, p. 33)

21. Engage in the anti-racist silence of learning. (REAL TALK, ACTION-NOW Learning Engagement, p. 34)

22. For BIPAL people: Engage in anti-racist protective silence. (REAL TALK, ACTION-NOW Learning Engagement, p. 35)

23. For white people: Refuse to engage in racist protective silence. (REAL TALK, ACTION-NOW Learning Engagement, p. 35)

24. Resist all uses of "thoughts and prayers" that perpetrate racism. (REAL TALK, ACTION-NOW Learning Engagement, p. 36)

25. Review all legal, procedural, and best practices language and policies for coded language that protects and entrenches racism. (REAL TALK, ACTION-NOW Learning Engagement, p. 37)

26. Identify the language that silences and omits the factors of systemic racism that create and sustain racial inequities. (REAL TALK, ACTION-NOW Learning Engagement, p. 37)

27. For BIPAL people: Create language and expose the specific ways that underlying systemic racism negatively and unequally burdens and harms BIPAL people and organizations. (REAL TALK, ACTION-NOW Learning Engagement, p. 37)

28. For white people: Unlearn the word share when redistributing money to enact racialized economic equity. Remember the phrase "You can't share what you steal." (REAL TALK, ACTION-NOW Learning Engagement, pp. 37-38)

29. Focus efforts on and ensure outcomes of racial equity, not racial equality. (REAL TALK, ACTION-NOW Learning Engagement, p. 38)

30. Prioritize racial justice over "order," "tradition," or "standards." (REAL TALK, ACTION-NOW Learning Engagement, p. 38)

31. Focus on structural racism, not the symptoms of racism, which often get us caught up in never-ending strategy sessions. (REAL TALK, ACTION-NOW Learning Engagement, p. 38)

32. Unlearn the word forgive for debt incurred based in white supremacist policies and practices. Use and enact the words reparations and redistribution instead. (REAL TALK, ACTION-NOW Learning Engagement, p. 38)

33. Challenge all policies that pressure BIPAL people to conform to and to internalize beauty standards of whiteness, which uphold racism. (REAL TALK, ACTION-NOW Learning Engagement, p. 39)

34. For white people, research, learn, and develop the skill set to identify company or organization descriptions that uphold white supremacy and racism. (REAL TALK, ACTION-NOW Learning Engagement, p. 39 action item and representative example to use for practice)

35. Disrupt white overtalking. (REAL TALK, ACTION-NOW Learning Engagement, p. 40)

36. For white people: Interrogate desire for burdening BIPAL people to teach us more anti-racism information. Interrogate need for more anti-racism information before anti-racist action. (REAL STRATEGIES, pp. 41-42)

37. Think about and use "entry points" instead of journey language in anti-racism work. (REAL STRATEGIES, pp. 42-43)

38. For white people, interrogate and remove all excuses for not doing the work of anti-racism right now. Ask, "What forms of racism still benefit me by this/that excuse?" and eliminate that. (REAL STRATEGIES, pp. 43-45)

39. For white people: Refuse to distance ourselves from our whiteness, the privileges we receive from racism, and the reality that we can't get from our whiteness to anti-racism work without external intervention of some sort. (REAL STRATEGIES, Michelle's Real Talk blue box, pp. 45-46)

40. Use to-do and not-to-do lists to enact anti-racism. Discern and refuse to enact the ways in which to-do and not-to-do lists perpetrate racism. (REAL STRATEGIES, pp. 46-47)

41. Interrogate responses to the wording, "white people doing the least amount of damage and racism" versus "white people doing the greatest amount of good in terms of anti-racism work." (REAL STRATEGIES, box, p. 47)

42. For white people: Build resilience against white manipulation (fragility). (REAL STRATEGIES, pp. 48-49 and Action Now Learning Experiment p. 57)

43. For BIPAL people: Recognize when resilience is needed, but build more and more resistance to white supremacy and racism. (REAL STRATEGIES, pp. 49-50)

44. Continually refute whitewashed history and testimonies that center and valorize white people, diminish and erase BIPAL people, and use codes to hide the realities of racism in all of its forms. (REAL STRATEGIES, pp. 50-51)

45. For BIPAL people: Interrogate your involvement (through witnessing, participating, or urging) in actions that perpetrated racialized harm against another BIPAL sibling. What did you gain or lose by doing so? What anti-racist act will you engage next time? (REAL STRATEGIES, response box, p. 52)

46. For white people: Interrogate emotional, intellectual, and physical responses to being instructed not to participate in an aspect of anti-racism, a meeting, a group, or a strategy session. What aspect of racism or white supremacy is connected to that? What do you need to do to dislodge it? (REAL STRATEGIES, response box, p. 52)

47. For BIPAL people: Refuse to denounce our thoughts, ideas, history, and ancestral teachings (or to accept white thoughts, value systems, religion, and mediocrity) in order to secure our advancement. (REAL STRATEGIES, p. 52)

48. For BIPAL people: Stop coddling white people's manipulation (fragility). (REAL STRATEGIES, pp. 52-53)

49. For white people: Identify how our white manipulation (fragility) has been coddled by others or by us. Name specifically how these actions perpetrate racism. Refer to strategies for building resilience against white manipulation (fragility) to eliminate any opportunity for coddling to occur. (REAL STRATEGIES, pp. 53-54)

50. For BIPAL people: Refuse to allow white people's manipulation (fragility) to influence which BIPAL leaders we groom, select, and value. (REAL STRATEGIES, pp. 54-55)

51. Refuse to use the crabs-in-a-barrel model to describe the reality that white supremacy pits BIPAL people against each other by using racialized discrimination to restrict access to funds, opportunities, positions, promotions, resources, and rights. (REAL STRATEGIES, pp. 54-55)

52. For BIPAL people: Refuse to accept and obey respectability politics. (REAL STRATEGIES, p. 55)

53. For BIPAL people: Commit to not coming to the rescue of white people when they are confronted with their own racism. Practice how you will do this ahead of time. (REAL STRATEGIES, ACTION-NOW Learning Engagement, p. 57)

54. For BIPAL people: Call out white manipulation (fragility). Do not coddle. (REAL STRATEGIES, ACTION-NOW Learning Engagement, p. 57)

55. For white people: Build resilience against our own white manipulation (fragility) by learning to manage our emotions and refuse to demand energy and attention that should be going toward anti-racism work. (REAL STRATEGIES, ACTION-NOW Learning Engagement, p. 57)

56. For white people: Build resilience against our white manipulation (fragility) by refusing to expect BIPAL people to care for us while we deal with the guilt, shame, and awareness of our racism. (REAL STRATEGIES, ACTION-NOW Learning Engagement, p. 57)

57. For white people: Build resilience against our white manipulation (fragility) by taking the time and effort necessary to learn how what we do or did is racist and what to do instead. (REAL STRATEGIES, ACTION-NOW Learning Engagement, p. 57)

58. Refuse to allow white manipulation (fragility) to be acceptable, ever. (REAL STRATEGIES, ACTION-NOW Learning Engagement, p. 57)

59. For BIPAL people: Honor BIPAL-only spaces by reserving the option to invite or not invite white people, and remember to give ourselves permission / allow ourselves to be in spaces where we have and utilize this option. (REAL STRATEGIES, ACTION-NOW Learning Engagement, p. 58)

60. For white people: Honor BIPAL-only spaces by paying close and careful attention to directions and descriptions of a gathering space to check whether it is a BIPAL-only space. (REAL STRATEGIES, ACTION-NOW Learning Engagement, p. 58)

61. For white people: Honor BIPAL-only spaces by learning and looking for wording (explicit) and coding (culturally specific language) that indicates a space is for BIPAL people only. (REAL STRATEGIES, ACTION-NOW Learning Engagement, p. 58)

62. For white people: Honor BIPAL-only spaces by learning about why BIPAL-only spaces are critical and how/why white people invading them perpetrates racism and white supremacy. (REAL STRATEGIES, ACTION-NOW Learning Engagement, p. 58)

63. For white people: Honor BIPAL-only spaces by attending if (and only if) invited by a BIPAL person. Speak only when asked, and be especially careful to obey instructions as to what they are asking for us to do or speak about. (REAL STRATEGIES, ACTION-NOW Learning Engagement, p. 58)

64. Do not create false equivalencies between BIPAL-only spaces and white segregated spaces. (REAL STRATEGIES, ACTION-NOW Learning Engagement, p. 58)

65. Do not create BIPAL-only spaces as an afterthought or add-on, or in less-than-desirable or less visible spaces. (REAL STRATEGIES, ACTION-NOW Learning Engagement, p. 58)

66. For BIPAL people: Remember that rest is an essential component of the resistance strategy we must create for ourselves. (REAL STRATEGIES, ACTION-NOW Learning Engagement, p. 59)

67. For white people: Do not create a false equivalency between our tiredness from doing anti-racism work that repudiates harm we've caused and the tiredness of BIPAL people who experience the body/mind/spirit/soul exhaustion from being direct targets of racism. (REAL STRATEGIES, ACTION-NOW Learning Engagement, p. 59)

68. Engage in racially positioned and balanced rest to promote the health necessary to continue to interrupt racism in REAL TIME. (REAL STRATEGIES, ACTION-NOW Learning Engagement, p. 59)

69. Avoid burnout and self-adulatory martyrdom—these are not anti-racist. (REAL STRATEGIES, ACTION-NOW Learning Engagement, p. 59)

70. For BIPAL people: Remember that we are the ones who are best capable of creating or cosigning strategies that actually disrupt, dislodge, and dismantle racism. (REAL STRATEGIES, ACTION-NOW Learning Engagement, p. 60)

71. For BIPAL people: Place value—monetary and otherwise—on the anti-racism strategies that we create and that white people use. (REAL STRATEGIES, ACTION-NOW Learning Engagement, p. 61)

72. For BIPAL people: Hold white allies/accomplices/people accountable for co-opting or plagiarizing the work of BIPAL people. (REAL STRATEGIES, ACTION-NOW Learning Engagement, p. 60)

73. For white people, follow this overarching template for anti-racism work: BIPAL people create or sign off on strategy, white people implement all work except that designated by BIPAL people for only BIPAL people to do, and white people hold themselves accountable to BIPAL people to determine correctness and faithfulness. (REAL STRATEGIES, ACTION-NOW Learning Engagement, p. 60)

74. For white people: Do not appropriate the words, work, or strategies of BIPAL people. (REAL STRATEGIES, ACTION-NOW Learning Engagement, p. 60)

75. For white people: Learn to recognize and name the interventions that have taught us to move from our own whiteness (in thought, beliefs, and actions) to anti-racism thought and work. Act accordingly. (REAL STRATEGIES, ACTION-NOW Learning Engagement, p. 60)

76. Teach strategies based in racial positionality. (REAL STRATEGIES, ACTION-NOW Learning Engagement, p. 60)

77. For BIPAL people: Transfer mortgages, business accounts, and personal accounts to Black-owned credit unions and banks. (REAL STRATEGIES, ACTION-NOW Learning Engagement, p. 65—ALSO SEE creating racial equity model/budget in REAL CHANGE ACTION-NOW Learning Engagement, p. 61)

78. Buy Black. (REAL STRATEGIES, ACTION-NOW Learning Engagement, p. 61—ALSO SEE creating racial equity model/budget in REAL CHANGE ACTION-NOW Learning Engagement, p. 97, 102-104)

79. For BIPAL people: Protect investments, invest in our communities, recognize our economic power, and refuse to undervalue our worth. (REAL STRATEGIES, ACTION-NOW Learning Engagement, p. 61—ALSO SEE creating racial equity model/budget in REAL CHANGE ACTION-NOW Learning Engagement, p. 97, 102-104)

80. For white people: Transfer all accounts, loans, mortgages, and credit card balances to BIPAL-owned institutions, and use our

social and leadership power in any organizations we belong to encourage them to transfer their accounts, mortgages, and loans similarly. (REAL STRATEGIES, ACTION-NOW Learning Engagement, p. 61—ALSO SEE creating racial equity model/budget in REAL CHANGE ACTION-NOW Learning Engagement, p. 97, 102-104)

81. For white people: Do not transfer money or accounts to Black- or BIPAL-owned credit unions—doing so could shift racialized ownership. (REAL STRATEGIES, ACTION-NOW Learning Engagement, p. 61—ALSO SEE creating racial equity model/budget in REAL CHANGE ACTION-NOW Learning Engagement, p. 97, 102-104)

82. Create economic racial equity. (REAL STRATEGIES, ACTION-NOW Learning Engagement, p. 61—ALSO SEE creating racial equity model/budget in REAL CHANGE ACTION-NOW Learning Engagement, p. 97, 102-104)

83. For BIPAL people: To decenter whiteness, resist recentering whiteness. (REAL STRATEGIES, ACTION-NOW Learning Engagements, p. 64)

84. For BIPAL people: To decenter whiteness, resist defending white manipulation (fragility). (REAL STRATEGIES, ACTION-NOW Learning Engagements, p. 64)

85. For BIPAL people: To decenter whiteness, resist conforming to white supremacy. (REAL STRATEGIES, ACTION-NOW Learning Engagements, p. 64)

86. For white people: To decenter whiteness, stop saying "I'm giving up my spot for BIPAL people" and say "I am stepping down; my staying reinforces and centers whiteness." (REAL STRATEGIES, ACTION-NOW Learning Engagements, p. 64)

87. For BIPAL people: remember we are not obligated to teach white people about racism. (REAL STRATEGIES, ACTION-NOW Learning Engagement, "Begging/Asking for help in Anti-Racism work," p. 62)

88. For white people: Refuse to demand help or instruction about racism and anti-racism from BIPAL people by interrogating all the words and body language we use in our requests. (REAL

STRATEGIES, ACTION-NOW Learning Engagement, "Begging/Asking for help in Anti-Racism work," p. 62)

89. For white people: Refuse to demand help or instruction about racism and anti-racism from BIPAL people by obeying their strategies and remembering that it is never their job to teach us. When they do, it is on their timeline, not ours. (REAL STRATEGIES, ACTION-NOW Learning Engagement, "Begging/Asking for help in Anti-Racism work," p. 62)

90. For white people: Refuse to demand help or instruction about racism and anti-racism from BIPAL people by critically assessing our language through the perspective of someone who is harmed by the injustice we want to learn about. Would we recoil if an abuser asked the person they abused for help using the same language we're using for our request? (REAL STRATEGIES, ACTION-NOW Learning Engagement, "Begging/Asking for help in Anti-Racism work," p. 62)

91. For BIPAL people: Resist buying into the white supremacy playbook that pits BIPAL people against each other as if our needs are mutually exclusive and leads us to compete against each other instead of actually dislodging white supremacy. (REAL STRATEGIES, ACTION-NOW Learning Engagement, p. 63)

92. For white people: Refuse to pit BIPAL people against each other by learning and exposing how white supremacy limits resources, access, opportunities, space, and respect for BIPAL people. (REAL STRATEGIES, ACTION-NOW Learning Engagement, p. 63)

93. For white people: Refuse to pit BIPAL people against each other by recognizing how white supremacy often creates separate and unequal buckets for "everyone" and BIPAL people, and that BIPAL people are only guided toward the latter while only white people are guided toward the former. (REAL STRATEGIES, ACTION-NOW Learning Engagement, p. 63)

94. For white people: Refuse to pit BIPAL people against each other by ensuring that information about all scholarships, grants, fellowships, jobs, promotions, and so on are shared with BIPAL-caucused or affinity groups in addition to what is considered "mainstream." (REAL STRATEGIES, ACTION-NOW Learning Engagement, p. 63)

95. Rename and redefine mainstream. (REAL STRATEGIES, ACTION-NOW Learning Engagement, p. 63)

96. Refuse to pit BIPAL people against each other by dismantling the lie of the zero-sum game, which insists that if one person or group has some, there is less for everyone else. Amplify also how equality models support the zero-sum game. (REAL STRATEGIES, ACTION-NOW Learning Engagement, p. 63)

97. Expose every way that white supremacy uses wording, policy, and practices to support the lie that white people deserve—and deserve the largest share of—resources, and how this creates rules that keep resources from BIPAL people. (REAL STRATEGIES, ACTION-NOW Learning Engagement, p. 63)

98. For BIPAL people: Elect, affirm, and empower our own leaders. (REAL STRATEGIES, ACTION-NOW Learning Engagement, p. 64)

99. For BIPAL people: Refuse to use what Audre Lorde called "the master's tools" to dismantle "the master's house." (REAL STRATEGIES, ACTION-NOW Learning Engagement, p. 64)

100. For white people: Obey BIPAL-selected leadership decisions. (REAL STRATEGIES, ACTION-NOW Learning Engagement, p. 64)

101. For white people: Obey BIPAL leaders and their leadership. (REAL STRATEGIES, ACTION-NOW Learning Engagement, p. 64)

102. For white people: Interrogate our first and second reactions to the word obey in number 100 and 101 above. (REAL STRATEGIES, ACTION-NOW Learning Engagement, p. 64)

103. For white people: Assess the racism and white supremacy behind any resistance to BIPAL leadership. (REAL STRATEGIES, ACTION-NOW Learning Engagement, p. 64)

104. For white people: Resist saying, "I agree with the goal, just not the tactics" when referencing BIPAL leaders, leadership, or strategies. (REAL STRATEGIES, ACTION-NOW Learning Engagement, p. 64)

105. Be able to recognize the tactics the logic system of racism uses to obstruct the urgent necessity and required skill sets to interrupt it in the moment. (REAL TIME, p. 65)

106. Refuse to say that some people "aren't ready" to do anti-racism. Replace that language with "Some people refuse to do the work of anti-racism." (REAL TIME, p. 65)

107. Learn about how the phrase "meet the people where they are" and "love the people" perpetrate and protect racism, and be able to teach this to someone else. (white people only teach other white people). REAL TIME, pp. 66-68)

108. Focus on outcomes, not intentions. (REAL TIME, pp. 66-67)

109. For white people: Refuse to allow our "I" statements, our opinions, or our heritage to serve as cover for racism. (REAL TIME, p. 67)

110. Never allow for white people's timeline or comfort to dictate or determine anti-racism strategies. (REAL TIME, p. 68)

111. Practice scripts for interrupting and dismantling racism that disparages Black women for speaking up about diversity in meetings, and prepare to enact them. Then do it. (REAL TIME, for white people p. 72, for all people p. 69)

112. For white people: Practice scripts for interrupting and dismantling racism that describes BIPAL candidates during a job search as "not fitting the organization's culture," and prepare to enact them. Then do it. (REAL TIME, pp. 69-70, 73-74)

113. For white people: Practice scripts for interrupting and dismantling racism occurring when white leaders disparage ideas and strategies created by BIPAL people only to steal them and take credit. Prepare to use your scripts. Then do it. (REAL TIME, pp. 70-71)

114. Be able to describe the differences between "calling out," "cancel culture," and "calling in" and how each works, or doesn't, to interrupt and dismantle racism. (REAL TIME, p. 71)

115. Address in public racism that has been perpetrated in public. (REAL TIME, pp. 72-73 and blue box p. 72 - SEE ALSO, #7, Matthew text interpretation)

116. Practice scripts to interrupt and dismantle the racism that emerges from intercultural competency workshops when difference is erased or racism is ignored for the sake of similarities, peace, or healing. Prepare to do use them. Then do it. (REAL TIME, pp. 74-75)

117. Practice scripts to interrupt and dismantle racism that occurs when BIPAL people's testimonies of racial harm are dismissed as "their experiences" or "opinions" and as not enough proof racism occurred. Prepare to use them. Then do it. (REAL TIME, pp. 75-76)

118. Learn (and enact) five things critical to interrupting and dismantling racism in REAL TIME. (REAL TIME, p. 77)

119. Name two ways you will overcome a personal hesitation toward interrupting racism in REAL TIME during the next week. Then ensure you do them. (REAL TIME, p. 78)

120. Attempt writing scripts to interrupt and dismantle racism in REAL TIME using five things from number 77. Four scenarios are included. (REAL TIME, pp. 79-82)

121. Name at least two things you can and will do to use your platform and whatever power you have to interrupt and dismantle racism. (REAL CHANGE, pp. 84-85)

122. Refuse to interpret BIPAL people naming the realities of systemic racism and discrimination as if they are excuses for limiting their survival and success. (REAL CHANGE, pp. 85-86)

123. For BIPAL people: Be actively anti-racist instead of relying on the fact that we cannot be racist because we do not have the systemic power to uphold or change policies. Practice refusing to do the bidding of whiteness, participate in racist behaviors, or advance the agendas and systems that perpetrate racialized terror. (REAL CHANGE, p. 85)

124. For BIPAL people: Name any excuses you have used that have prevented you from using your opportunities or platforms to make an anti-racist difference. (REAL CHANGE, p. 86)

125. For white people: Name any excuses you have made to literally excuse yourself from engaging in anti-racism work. What will you do to counter these excuses—beyond simply saying you will not use them again? (REAL CHANGE, p. 86)

126. Think of an anti-racism act that you have participated in (or heard about) and identify, name, locate, describe, and explain with proven evidence that racism has been interrupted and/ or dismantled. If you cannot, what would need to be different

about the action in order for anti-racism to actually occur? (REAL CHANGE, p. 87)

127. For white people: What proof or evidence can be externally verified of your anti-racism work? Avoid all temptation to include anything about your intentions, your promises, or your uncertainties. (REAL CHANGE, p. 87)

128. Name at least one specific anti-racism action (one that has proven external evidence of interrupting or dismantling racism) that emerged from your last anti-racism knowledge-gathering experience (such as a book study, workshop). (REAL CHANGE, p. 88)

129. Evaluate how many anti-racism strategies from this book (or this list) you have enacted since you began reading Anti-Racism 4REALS. (REAL CHANGE, p. 88—ALSO read the rest of this list ☺)

130. Imagine you are proposing the creation an anti-racism strategy or culture in your organization. Consider the following sentence: "REAL CHANGE requires a sustainable revolution in policies, procedures, power, and practice." How would you paraphrase this to teach the decision makers what is required for anti-racism work to actually happen? (REAL CHANGE, p. 91)

131. Use this appendix to answer the prompts in the "Real List 4 REAL CHANGE" templates to create action plans and accountability for interrupting and dismantling racism. (REAL CHANGE, pp. 92-96)

132. Develop an equity model. Start with ten prompt questions and research any additional information or skill sets needed to enact it. (REAL CHANGE, p. 97)

133. Develop an anti-racist strategy for creating a more racially diverse board or leadership Group. Then do it. (REAL CHANGE, pp. 98-101)

134. Create an anti-racist budget. Then use and honor it. (REAL CHANGE, pp. 102-104)

135. Compare your scripts from number 120 to the author-created scripts for the same four scenarios and determine if your scripts perpetrate racism in any way. If yes, correct them. If no, prepare to enact them or strategies from them. (APPENDIX A, pp. 113-116)

136. Utilize the REAL TIME author-created scripts in Appendix A. (pp. 113-116)

137. Contact 4REALS: Anti-Racist Anti-Racism Training and Consulting, LLC for more information and upcoming workshops, and to schedule anti-racism consulting or training. www.antiracism-4REALS.com

BIBLIOGRAPHY

Baldwin, James. "The Black Scholar Interviews James Baldwin." *Conversations with James Baldwin*. Edited by F. R. Standley and L.H. Pratt. Jackson, MS: University of Mississippi Press, 1989.

Beckford, Sheila, Tiffany French-Goffe, Richard Hayes, Dorlimar Lebron Malavé and Laurel Scott. "Open Letter to Bishop Bickerton." Black Methodists for Church Renewal NYAC. July 30, 2020. https://docs.google.com/forms/d/e/1FAIpQLSflQML5L95LWs3zw5m2CRSSfqxPJKkIINSPQ1b-bQWaGSwjyLQ/viewform.

Brueggemann, Walter. *Interrupting Silence*. Louisville: Westminster John Knox Press, 2018.

Cobb, James C. "Even Though He Is Revered Today, MLK Was Widely Disliked by the American Public When He Was Killed." *Smithsonian Magazine*. April 4, 2018. https://www.smithsonianmag.com/history/why-martin-luther-king-had-75-percent-disapproval-rating-year-he-died-180968664.

DiAngelo, Robin. *White Fragility: Why It's So Hard for White People to Talk About Racism*. Boston: Beacon Press, 2018.

Howard University Rankin Chapel. "Sermon, Cornel West." You Tube video, 1:00.01. April 17, 2011. https://www.youtube.com/watch?v=nGqP7S_WO6o.

King, Martin Luther Jr. *Letter from Birmingham Jail*. Penguin Modern. London, England: Penguin Classics, 2018.

King, Regina, director. 2020. "One Night in Miami." Amazon Studios.

Lake, Philip S. "Resistance, Resilience and Restoration." *Ecological Management and Restoration* 14, no. 1 (2012): 20–24. https://doi.org/10.1111/emr.12016

Lorde, Audre. "The Master's Tools Will Never Dismantle The Master's House." In *Sister Outsider: Essays and Speeches by Audre Lorde*, 110-113. Berkeley: Crossing Press, 2007.

_____. "The Transformation of Silence into Language and Action." In *Sister Outsider: Essays and Speeches by Audre Lorde*, 40–44. Berkeley: Crossing Press, 2007.

Stack, Liam. "Ben Carson Refers to Slaves as 'Immigrants' in First Remarks to HUD Staff." *The New York Times*. March 6, 2017. https://www.nytimes.com/2017/03/06/us/politics/ben-carson-refers-to-slaves-as-immigrants-in-first-remarks-to-hud-staff.html.

Reagon, Bernice Johnson. "Ella's Song: We Who Believe in Freedom Cannot Rest Until It Comes." Performed by Sweet Honey in the Rock. 1981. http://thue.standford.edu/jacquie/songs/ella.html.

Tutu, Desmond. *Oxford Essential Quotations*, 5th edition. Oxford University Press, online version 2017. https://www.oxfordreference.com/view/10.1093/acref.

United Methodist Church. *The Book of Discipline of the United Methodist Church*. Nashville United Methodist Publishing House, 2016.

Workplace Fairness. "Hair and Grooming Discrimination." Accessed January 1, 2021. https://www.workplacefairness.org/hair-discrimination.